SAMOTHRAC

Photo Nicholas D. Ohly
Frontispiece. View of Palaiopolis, with the Gattilusi Citadel in the Foreground.

INSTITUTE OF FINE ARTS, NEW YORK UNIVERSITY

SAMOTHRACE

A Guide to the
EXCAVATIONS AND THE MUSEUM

By Karl Lehmann

Sixth edition, revised and enlarged

Thessaloniki 1998

Library of Congress catalogue card number: 55-8563

Editorial work: I. M. Akamatis

Preface

This little book has been written to guide the visitor and student who come to Samothrace. I have attempted to make it understandable to the layman and useful to the student of antiquity. The result, I realize, may not be wholly satisfactory to either. But in the years to come, before the scholarly work resulting from our excavations and now in preparation is available, it may fill a gap.

In accordance with the purpose of this guide, no references to ancient authors, inscriptions, or details of archaeological evidence have been given. The description of the excavations and the Museum is limited to essentials. For details and documentation, the reader may find certain leads in the short, very selective bibliography. The statements on the religion of the Great Gods, even after the profuse new evidence obtained in our excavations, touch upon highly controversial topics of the history of religion. I have given my personal views on those matters; and the reader should remember that although all are based on evidence either literary, epigraphical, or archaeological, that evidence in some instances might allow different interpretation.

The excavations, the exhibition in the Museum, and the scholarly results which are the basis of this book could not have been achieved without the energy, spirit, and intelligence of my collaborators —archaeologists and architects alike— who over the years have been too numerous to be mentioned individually. But, among them, special homage must be paid in this guidebook to my wife, Phyllis Williams Lehmann, who has transformed the Sanctuary from a wilderness with ruins into a major archaeological site and created order out of chaos. A special acknowledgment, too, is here due to the generous sponsors of our work, the Bollingen Foundation, and to a private donor, who have enabled us to create the Museum. Finally, I should say that splendid workmen, led by the indispensable Georgios Nikolaides, have performed miracles in a relatively short time and that Greek authorities and colleagues as well as the directors of the American School of Classical Studies at Athens have always been most helpful.

Samothrace, August 1954

Karl Lehmann

Preface to the Second Edition

This revised edition includes changes and additions in text and illustrations owing to the progress of our work, among them partial restoration of the façade of the Hieron, excavations in the southern cemetery and work on the final publication. In all these endeavors, the sponsors and helpers referred to in the preface of the first edition have continued to assist us.

The publication of this second edition and its availability at a reduced price have been made possible by the financial support of an anonymous philanthropic foundation.

Haydenville, Massachusetts
December 1959

Karl Lehmann

Preface to the Third Edition

Karl Lehmann's original text for the first edition of the Guide remains the basis of the third edition. It has been revised to incorporate corrections resulting from our continuing work on the final publication and enlarged to include finds from the South Nekropolis, now exhibited in Hall D of the enlarged Museum, as well as preliminary descriptions of the buildings on the eastern and western hills of the Sanctuary that are currently being excavated.

I have not altered previous statements about buildings which require further study (e.g. the Anaktoron), preferring to modify the second edition only where our investigations have now been completed.

I am greatly indebted to Elsbeth B. Dusenbery, Iris C. Love, and James R. McCredie for their contributions to this edition, in particular, for revising the descriptions of Halls B and C of the Museum and for providing descriptions of Hall D and the new areas of the excavation.

Haydenville, Massachusetts
March 1966

Phyllis Williams Lehmann

Preface to the Fourth Edition

Karl Lehmann's original text for the first edition of the *Guide* continues to be the basis of the fourth edition. Once again, both its text and its illustrations have been revised and enlarged to incorporate corrections, resulting from our continuing work on the final publication, in particular, our further excavation of buildings on the eastern and western hills of the Sanctuary (the dedication of Philip III Arrhidaios and Alexander IV, the Stoa, the structures below the Byzantine fortification and their vicinities) and our further investigation of the Temenos and its Propylon and the Propylon of Ptolemy II.

Again, I have not altered previous statements about areas in the Sanctuary that require further study, preferring to modify the third edition only where our investigations have been completed. Recent advances in our knowledge of ceramics and other evidence upon which the pre-Classical chronology of the Double Precinct and the Anaktoron had been based may necessitate substantial revision of their dates. Thorough study of these and related problems has now been undertaken. Pending its completion, no change in the previous discussion of these monuments has been introduced.

I am especially indebted to Elsbeth Dusenbery and James R. McCredie for their contributions to this volume, in particular, for Mrs. Dusenbery's careful revision of Chapter IV: The Museum, and to Mr. McCredie for his extensive additions to Chapter III: The Excavations, in which we have both been aided by Alfred K. Frazer. John Kurtich has provided a new series of plans of the island, the Sanctuary, and the Museum, with the help of Ioannis M. Akamatis, that we trust will render the *Guide* of increased use to visitors. To all these faithful collaborators, I am most grateful.

Haydenville, Massachusetts
December 1973

Phyllis Williams Lehmann

Preface to the Fifth Edition

Karl Lehmann's original text for the first edition of the *Guide* continues to be the basis of the fifth edition. Chapters I and II remain virtually unchanged. However, Chapter III: The Excavations, reflects reinvestigation of the Anaktoron and the structures below it, the Sacristy, and the Rotunda of Arsinoe which has led to a different interpretation and a new chronology for these buildings. Once again, both the text and the illustrations of this chapter have been revised and enlarged to incorporate corrections resulting from our continuing work on the final publication, in particular, renewed study of the Rotunda of Arsinoe. Pending final publication of Volume 7 which will be devoted to that building, we are adding three new reconstructions of the Rotunda drawn by John Kurtich based on solutions provided by James R. McCredie. Further excavation of both the eastern and western hills of the Sanctuary has yielded new buildings which have been included in the description of these areas.

I am especially indebted to James R. McCredie for his extensive additions and alterations of Chapter III. Elsbeth Dusenbery has again revised sections of Chapter IV: The Museum, and Ioannis M. Akamatis, as a result of his Greek translation of the fourth edition of the English *Guide*, has provided numerous corrections. To all of these faithful collaborators, I am, once again, most grateful.

Haydenville, Massachusetts
January 1983

Phyllis Williams Lehmann

Preface to the Sixth Edition

Karl Lehmann's original text for the first edition of the *Guide* continues to be the basis of the sixth edition. Chapters I and II remain virtually unchanged. However, Chapter III: The Sanctuary of the Great Gods, reflects new excavations and reinvestigation of several monuments. Once again, both the text and the illustrations of this chapter have been revised and enlarged to incorporate corrections resulting from our continuing work on the final publication.

I am especially indebted to John Kurtich, who has provided new drawings, to Demetri Matsas, who has provided information on the important excavations of the Service of Antiquities, to Ioannis M. Akamatis, who has aided this project in every way, to Phyllis Williams Lehmann, who has read and improved the entire text, and to student members of the staff, especially Lisa Brody and Rachel Kousser, but also others too numerous to acknowledge individually, who have removed many errors and infelicities from this book. To all of these faithful collaborators, I am most grateful.

Palaiopolis, Samothrace
June, 1996

James R. McCredie

Table of Contents

List of Illustrations

Photo Nicholas D. Ohly
Fig. 1. View of the Southern Coast.

I

The Island and Its History

The island of Samothrace forms a landmark in the northeastern Aegean. Its forbidding mountains, rising abruptly from the sea to a height of 5,459 feet at the Peak of the Moon (Mt. Phengari), dominate the landscape of eastern Thrace and the Thracian archipelago (Fig. 1). Spectacular in scenery even among the many beautiful islands of Greece, it is modest in size, having but a small, if fertile, coastal plain in the north, a richer rolling country in the west and southwest. It has today few resources to support a population of fewer than 4,000 inhabitants. Wild goats still roam the mountains as they did in antiquity. Herds of goats and sheep form the main livestock. Grain is sparse. But fruit is abundant and excellent and Samothracian onions, large in size, were exported even in antiquity. In the days of Homer, the then densely-

15

wooded island was probably much more fertile. There are indications that natural iron ore occurred in some areas and was exploited from early times. A black "stone" of very light weight was used and exported for personal ornaments. Even now, after many centuries of deforestation and erosion, there is an abundance of springs and good water. Hot sulphur springs, frequented in summer for medical cures at least since Byzantine times, are found at Loutra in the center of the northern part of the island. But there never was a good natural harbor. Today the only small harbor, Kamariotissa, is at the western tip of the island. From it a paved road leads to the main village, Chora, hidden in the folds of the barren mountain slopes; another road leads to Xeropotamo, Lakoma (whence a gravel road runs to Ammos Beach), and Prophetes Elias in the southwestern part of the island; and a third follows the northern coast to Palaiopolis and its archaeological zone, to Loutra, and eastward to the beach at Kepos, where steep cliffs make the south coast inaccessible. On the northern shore there were, in ancient times, a few small inlets now filled with sand. One such inlet near plentiful springs —now in a grove of ancient plane trees— attracted Greek settlers; and here on the site today called Palaiopolis (The Old City) they built their city, attaching it to a craggy promontory the top of which formed the akropolis (Frontispiece).

The island was more fertile then than it is now, but life was always hard in this wild mountain landscape. The sea is rough and stormy in these parts, with sharp winds blowing onto it from the Balkan highlands. Local winds falling down rapidly from the mountains soar through the valleys with sudden mad bursts. Winters are hard, with heavy rains and masses of snow at times covering even the plains and coasts.

If nature provided but scarce resources except for timber and fish, the island was privileged in its situation on a sea lane leading from Greece to the Dardanelles and the Black

Fig. 2. Prehistoric Cups from Kariotes.

Sea. In a region generally devoid of natural harbors, its mountain bulk, visible from afar, attracted sailors to take refuge in the small shelters of its northwestern shores. In times of extensive movements of people and goods along that lane by means of simple sailing ships, Samothrace was a natural center of importance, from the Greek colonization of the eighth and seventh centuries B.C. into the early Christian era. Halfway between Mt. Ida, which dominates the Dardanelles from above Troy, and Mt. Athos, the beacon on the other side of the Thracian sea that leads the sailor towards northern Greece, Samothrace was always the natural point of attraction and guidance to the colonist, the skipper, the merchant and the traveler.

The earliest phases of civilization on Samothrace are only now beginning to be explored by the Greek Archaeological Service; a description of these excavations may be found in Chapter V. Sporadic finds indicate that the island was inhabited in the Neolithic Age. A rich deposit of crude handmade pottery dating from the Bronze Age (second millennium B.C.) was discovered by peasants in 1939 in the district of Kariotes to the east of Palaiopolis (Museum Case C1, Fig. 2) and a chance find made in the Sanctuary long ago, an ax-shaped amulet, leads its history back to that period. Greek

Fig. 3. Handmade Local Ware. Seventh Century B.C.

writers claimed that the indigenous population of Samothrace had sprung from the earth earlier than any other people of Greece. Actually, it is probable that here, as elsewhere,
various tribes succeeded each other and mingled from the
Stone Age to the Iron Age in the early centuries of the last
millennium B.C.

The latest stratum of this pre-Greek population seems to
have belonged to the large family of Thracian people which
at the dawn of history dominated the southeastern part of
the Balkan peninsula. They survive in the legendary tradition of history found in ancient writers. They have left their
traces in fundamental concepts of the Samothracian religion.
Their non-Greek language was still used in the first century
B.C. as a ritual language of the cult. Documents of this language inscribed on a stone stele and on clay vessels dating
from the sixth through the fourth centuries B.C. have been
found in the excavations (Museum Case C11, see Figs. 69,
70).

The actual survival of this language, as well as the evident
pre-Greek elements in the Samothracian religion and the
mixture of fine Greek and crude native ceramics found together in the Sanctuary in a deposit of the seventh century
B.C. (Museum Cases C1 and C3, Fig. 3 and see Fig. 62), in-

dicate that Greek colonists arriving about 700 B.C. mingled peacefully with and blended their civilization with that of the natives.

Some ancient writers derived these colonists from Samos and dated their arrival centuries earlier. But the archaeological evidence contradicts this tradition, which was probably invented to account for the similarity of names; Homer called Samothrace the Thracian Samos. A fragment of an inscribed stele of the fourth century B.C. suggests that the Samothracian Greek dialect was "Aeolian" rather than "Ionian" and points to the origin of the settlers in northwestern Anatolia or Lesbos, regions closely related to Samothrace by legend and archaeological evidence alike. The settlers built their town in Palaiopolis (Frontispiece, see Fig. 23), the center of a Greek city-state comprising the entire island. They probably were ruled by a king whose title *Basileus* later survived, here as elsewhere in Greece, in that of their chief magistrate. The citizens were organized in five tribes. Their patron goddess was Athena —as in most Aeolian towns— whose sanctuary seems to have been located on the upper slopes of the town. At the same time, they began to develop and elaborate the native cult in the nearby Sanctuary.

Undoubtedly profiting from the wide framework of cultural and economic life that developed with the Greek colonization of the Archaic period and from its privileged geographical location, Samothrace rapidly became a major Greek city. Early among such cities, it had its own fine silver coinage in the sixth century B.C. with the image of Athena on the obverse (Museum Case B2). By that time, the town had a vast extent, never to be surpassed, as is indicated by Archaic tombs discovered to the west of it when the Xenia Hotel was constructed in this region, and it seems that large sections of one of the most conspicuous city walls of Greece (Fig. 4, see Fig. 23) date from the sixth century. By the end of the Archaic age, at the beginning of the fifth century, the

Photo Nicholas D. Ohly
Fig. 4. Postern in the City Wall.

Samothracians owned a *Peraia* on the Thracian seashore opposite the island between the city of Maroneia and the Thracian peninsula dominated by Ainos. It included several small towns, among them what is today Alexandroupolis. They thus virtually controlled the sea lane leading to the Dardanelles and had their own navy which contributed a small contingent to the battle of Salamis. In the same Archaic age of the sixth and early fifth centuries, the Sanctuary was adorned with conspicuous buildings, among them the Hall of Votive Gifts and the predecessors of the Hieron and, presumably, of the Anaktoron.

But, like certain other island states, Samothrace was rendered rather powerless during the ascendancy of strong new forces in the fifth century B.C. She became one of the many members of the Athenian empire, and fifty years later her advocate in Athens pleaded for a reduced assessment of tribute in view of the poverty of the island which lacked the resources of other, more privileged, members of the league. Samothrace, in this phase of Greek history, became a minor city.

Yet the fame of the Sanctuary and its mystery religion gave to the island a special character and importance. Increasingly the Sanctuary attracted visitors and became widely known. A profusion of literary documents referring to its cult and debating its nature emerged in the Classical age and continued throughout antiquity into the Christian era. Herodotus was initiated in the Sanctuary, as was the Spartan king Lysander. Aristophanes refers to the mysteries of Samothrace, implying that not infrequently members of his Attic audience had been initiated there. Plato, it seems, repeatedly alludes to them with reverence. To this period belong the stepped circular area at the entrance to the Sanctuary and the Orthostate Structure, a new building for *myesis*, initiation into the first stage of the mysteries. The royal house of Macedon had a special allegiance to the cult. It is reported that prince Philip first saw Olympias, a princess from Epirus, later mother of Alexander the Great, on the occasion of his initiation and immediately fell in love with her.

Samothrace thus became an unrivaled center of religious life in a large region extending from northern Greece through Macedonia and Thrace to northwestern Asia Minor. The special allegiance of the Macedonians to the gods of Samothrace in the age of Philip and Alexander continued in the royal patronage of Alexander's successors. Splendid buildings arose in rapid succession within a century and a half, most, if not all, of them due to the munificence of Philip's family and the Diadochs: the Hall of Choral Dancers (*ca.* 340 B.C.); the Altar Court probably dedicated by Alexander's half-brother and successor Arrhidaios (*ca.* 340-330 B.C.); the Hieron (the so-called New Temple, *ca.* 325 B.C.); a Doric building on the Eastern Hill dedicated by Arrhidaios, after his accession to the throne as Philip III, and his co-ruler, Alexander IV, the infant son of Alexander (between 323 and 317 B.C.); a small Doric Rotunda (*ca.* 350-300 B.C.); the Rotunda of Arsinoe (between 287 and 281 B.C. or between 276 and 270 B.C.); the monumental Propylon donated by Ptolemy II (between 285 and 281 B.C.); a huge stoa to shelter the crowds of visitors; a *neorion* to house the dedication of a warship (*ca.* 250 B.C.); a theater, banqueting halls, and a monumental ship-monument dominated by the famous Hellenistic sculpture known as the Victory of Samothrace (all between 300 and 150 B.C.) (Fig. 5). In addition to these ambitious structures, other magnificent votive gifts of "the kings" and in their honor were dedicated in the Sanctuary; for example, the colossal statue of Philip V that, together with the Doric column on which it stood, was dedicated by the Macedonians about 200 B.C. (see pp. 106, 163).

But Samothrace, an ever-growing center of religious tradition and prestige, was also strategically important in the fourth century B.C. and during the Hellenistic period, being used as naval base and stronghold by the second Athenian League, by King Lysimachos of Thrace, and by the Ptolemies, Seleucids, and Macedonians in turn. She no longer was a power in her own right but shielded herself behind the claim that the entire island was divine property, and even her possessions on the Thracian mainland were called in due time "the sacred land". Yet she must have continued to have her small navy, since the prow of a warship appears on her

Fig. 5. Paris, The Louvre: The Victory of Samothrace.
Early Second Century B.C.

coins early in the Hellenistic age. During this age, too, the old city walls were restored and assumed the final form still visible in impressive ruins.

Given its sacrosanct character, the island was considered a safe refuge for political exiles. One of them was the last Macedonian king, Perseus, who after his defeat by the Romans fled to Samothrace (168 B.C.) and was seized there in a dramatic episode of world history.

In all these upheavals of a turbulent age, the island evidently had a flourishing life, as the ruins and finds from this time show. Considerable economic assets to the island were both the great festivals, to which delegations from many Greek towns, primarily in northern Greece and Asia Minor, annually came and visitors to the Sanctuary who sought and obtained initiation throughout the summer months from April to September. It was in this period that the island produced the founder of scientific philology, Aristarchos. And a sculptor from Samothrace, Hieronymus, was successful in Rhodes, one of the great centers of art in this age.

Numerous writers discussed and debated the origin and character of the Samothracian religion. The Romans, at the time when they conquered Greece and built their empire, showed a special interest in this center of Greek religious life. The legend that Dardanos, the founder of the Trojan kingdom, had come from Samothrace and that Aeneas, his descendant, had brought the island's ancient cult to Rome gave Samothrace a peculiar interest to the Romans. From the end of the second century B.C. onward, as documents show, an ever-increasing stream of Roman pilgrims came to Samothrace, and this movement reached its climax in the late Republic. Men like Varro and Piso, the father-in-law of Caesar, Roman administrators and high-ranking officials appear among the initiates.

The Sanctuary and the island thus flourished, though in 84 B.C. the former was badly looted by the pirates who then infested the Aegean. Excavation in the Sanctuary has also revealed that early in the Empire a major catastrophe, probably an earthquake, caused havoc and led to extensive restorations and, in the case of the Anaktoron, a complete replacement. After this event, a sweeping remodeling took place, possibly as a result of Roman patronage. Subsequent calamities, again apparently natural, occasioned radical revisions to the structures on the Eastern and Western Hills.

During the Roman empire the same state of affairs prevailed. Apart from its importance as a religious center, Samothrace continued to be a natural stopping point on the shipping lanes that led from western Asia Minor and the Black Sea to northern Greece. St. Paul stayed there on his way to Neapolis (Kavalla), and it is possible that an Early Christian church built centuries later at the edge of the ancient harbor and discovered in 1938 commemorated that event. Among the many visitors of the imperial age was the Emperor Hadrian.

Nothing is known about the history of the town in later antiquity. The Sanctuary continued to flourish, and its popularity remained undiminished in the ancient world down to the third century. A decline began in that age. Yet the ancient religion continued in practice well into the Christian era and seems to have been forced out of existence only in the late fourth century after Christ.

Even within the general upheaval of that age, this must have been a deadly blow to the old island state. Its later history became shrouded in almost complete obscurity. It remained part of the Eastern Empire. Ravaged by pirates and eventually becoming their hideout, shaken by earthquakes and deprived of resources by progressive deforestation and erosion, it began to sink into oblivion. The process was slow and extended over many centuries. The ruins of numerous Christian churches, mostly small in size, are found all over the island, as are traces of a population which was

Fig. 6. View of Chora.

still dense in the early Byzantine era. Even in the sixth century, a large bath establishment of Roman type still functioned and was restored in the southwestern village of Alonia. A more rapid decline began in the eighth century. The harbor of the ancient town probably became unusable about that time through being sanded. The town itself, however, remained inhabited, if sparsely so, well into the fifteenth century. Ultimately, only one small ancient settlement survived to the west of it, in what is today the hamlet of Palaiopolis (around the Museum). The site retained military importance, and in the tenth century an imposing fort, presumably to serve a small garrison, was constructed on the northern terrace of the Western Hill. In response to unsettled times, the civilian population sought shelter inland, moving to a hidden place protected by a hill fortress of Byzantine origin, today the site of Chora (Fig. 6).

In the twilight of the Byzantine empire, the Emperor

Johannes VIII handed the island over to the Italian overlord of Ainos, Palamede Gattilusio, who ruled it by means of a Greek prefect. The Gattilusi built the castle of Chora into a strong fortress, the conspicuous ruins of which are still preserved, and protected the northern shore by another fortress on the site of the ancient town (Frontispiece). Its ruined towers, largely built of marble spoils from the glorious ancient sanctuary nearby, today form a romantic and melancholy landmark. Another such tower was built on the northeastern seashore at the beach of Phonias.

It was at this time that western explorers began to be interested in Samothrace. In 1419 the Italian Buondelmonte visited the island while charting the Aegean. More important was the visit in October 1444 of the humanist-merchant and diplomat, Cyriacus of Ancona, the first to revive interest in the history of ancient Samothrace (see Museum Hall B, Fig. 7).

Photo Oxford, Bodleian Library

Fig. 7. Inscribed Stele Drawn by Cyriacus of Ancona in 1444 (Oxford, Bodleian Library, Ms. Lat. Misc. d. 85, fol. 140r).

27

The Turkish conqueror of Constantinople drew on the population of Samothrace to resettle his depleted capital. Then the island fell into nearly complete oblivion. No historical records whatsoever exist for the three hundred years from 1500 to 1800.

Politically insignificant, economically poor, the island fell back into the quiet remoteness of primitive life. And this continued almost to the present, here and there interrupted by cruel bleeding in the conflicts between Greeks and Turks in 1821 and, again, during the Balkan wars of the early twentieth century until, in 1912, Samothrace was reunited with Greece.

Before that, however, the western world had grown increasingly interested in the island. Fascination with the tradition of its ancient mysteries loomed large in the learned books of western scholars of the seventeenth, eighteenth, and early nineteenth centuries. During the latter century, learned visitors began to come to the island and to report on its antiquities. The discovery of the Victory of Samothrace (Fig. 5) by the French Consul Champoiseau in 1863 was followed by intense studies and partial excavations by French (1866) and Austrian (1873-1875) scholars. Scholarly research of this kind was followed up from time to time in the late nineteenth and early twentieth centuries. In 1938 New York University began exploration and excavation of the main part of the Sanctuary. During the Second World War, Samothrace, its population and its antiquities suffered badly under Bulgarian military rule. But since the war, a new life has begun. The excavations were resumed in 1948 and work has been continued thereafter annually. Roads have been built, communications and lodging improved, and a museum has been constructed and installed by the American expedition. Samothrace is now again, as in antiquity, host to an ever increasing throng of visitors from far and near.

II

The Religion of the Great Gods

What constituted the major glory of ancient Samothrace and made it eminent among Greek cities was its cult of the Great Gods, as they were officially called. This cult included "mysteries", which were believed to be of venerable origin, and the initiation into them was no less renowned among the Greeks and Romans than that of Eleusis. But in Samothrace, participation in the mysteries was not necessarily required of those who came to the Sanctuary of the Gods as it was in Eleusis. The Sanctuary, like other public sanctuaries of Greece, was open to all for the worship of the Gods in whatever public form. At the same time, it was not strictly an official sanctuary of the Greek city-state, although situated very close to the ancient city. This is evident from the fact that the city itself was represented by ambassadors at the annual festivals as were foreign states. Like the sanctuaries of Delphi and Olympia, among others, the Sanctuary of Samothrace had an international character.

As was common in such sanctuaries, a plurality of divinities was grouped around a major figure. In Samothrace this figure was a "Great Mother" whose image, seated and attended by a lion, appears on many Samothracian coins

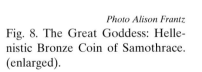

Photo Alison Frantz
Fig. 8. The Great Goddess: Hellenistic Bronze Coin of Samothrace. (enlarged).

29

Photo Anna Wachsmann
Fig. 9. Iron Ring from a Tomb.

(Fig. 8) as a counterpart to the head of the city patroness Athena. She was related to the Great Mother of Anatolia, the Phrygian Kybele, and to the Trojan Mother of Mount Ida. An all-powerful ruler of a wild, mountainous world, she was worshipped at sacred rocks where sacrifices were brought to her, as the excavations have revealed. In Samothrace these altars are big natural outcroppings of colorful porphyry rock, varying from green and red to blue and gray.

A curious feature of the cult of the Mother of the Rocks here is that she manifested her power, which was immanent in stones, in lodestones of magnetic iron of which rings were fashioned (Fig. 9), seemingly in the Sanctuary. Worn by the worshippers, they were associated by them with the Great Goddess (Museum Cases B1 and D5).

She was of pre-Greek origin and her worship in the Sanctuary preceded the advent of the Greeks. She was called Axieros in the native language, while the Greek settlers identified her with their earth-mother Demeter. It is also probable that the Greeks early called her Elektra, the Shining One, and Strategis, the Leader, though later Elektra became a legendary heroine.

It seems likely that in Samothrace the cults of two other great goddesses of nature, Hekate, with the non-Greek name Zerynthia, and Aphrodite Zerynthia, were split off from that of the old Mother of the Rocks, again invoked by the Greeks with different and familiar names. Aphrodite Zerynthia may be represented in curious three-breasted, naked idols found in a late Hellenistic tomb (Case C10, Fig. 10), and she may have been the goddess whose image appeared in a famous group by Skopas (see p. 76).

Attached to the Great Mother and possibly her subordinate spouse was an ithyphallic fertility god called Kadmilos by the natives of the Thracian archipelago and identified by the Greeks with their Hermes. The head of his sacred animal, the ram, together with his staff, the kerykeion, appear on Samothracian bronze coins of smaller denomination (Museum Case B2).

The kerykeion is incised on the inscribed stele from the Anaktoron (Hall A, Fig. 11) between two additional snakes symbolizing two attendant demons, who were represented by bronze statues in the same place as nude ithyphallic youths raising their hands in an old gesture of epiphany. In Samothrace these youths were called Kabeiroi, a name that is attached to such demons of varying number and age in many places. The Greeks identified the twins of Samothrace with their own twin gods, the Dioskouroi. Their symbols were snakes and stars, which occurred together on a silver ring found in Samothrace in 1939 and stolen during the war (see photograph in Museum Case B1). Again, it seems probable that the brothers Dardanos and Eëtion, bearing pre-Greek names and surviving in legends as the hero-founders of the Samothracian mysteries, were originally identical with

Photo Alison Frantz
Fig. 10. Terracotta Statuette from a Tomb. First Century B.C.

Photo Anna Wachsmann

Fig. 11. Bilingual Marble Stele Found in the
Anaktoron. Early Imperial.

the two Kabeiroi-Dioskouroi.

This group of divinities, the Great Mother Axieros, the
fertility god Kadmilos, and the demons, the Kabeiroi, seems
to form a unit of pre-Greek origin. But the Great Gods
included two more powerful figures: an underworld god and
his spouse, whom the Greeks called by the familiar names of
Hades and Persephone.

We know their names in the native language, too; in that idiom they were invoked as Axiokersos and Axiokersa. Inasmuch as this language survived in actual use for centuries after the Hellenization of Samothrace, the existence of these names does not preclude the possibility that this divine couple, rulers of the netherworld, was imported to Samothrace by the Greek colonists. They appear in images found in the excavations (Museum Case B1) as a bearded man (Fig. 12) and a young goddess with a peculiarly thin headgear (a variety of *polos*). The latter seems also to have been represented as a statue of a half-iconic type well known from Anatolia (Museum Case B1).

The familiar legend of the rape of the fertility goddess by the underworld god formed part of a sacred drama in the Samothracian festival. But in later times, the action of this rite was identified with the legendary story of the wedding of Kadmos and Harmonia, possibly because of the relationship of the name Kadmos to Kadmilos and of the appelative Elektra. This name, if used in Samothrace for the native Great Mother identified with Demeter, the mother of Persephone, might easily have led to such a fusion.

Fig. 12. Votive Terracotta of the Underworld God. Late Hellenistic.

The above conclusions may be drawn from what we now know about the nature of the divinities together worshipped as the Great Gods of Samothrace. It is probable that the public rites were those more or less common to all Greek sanctuaries: sacrifices of animal —scattle, sheep, and pigs (to the underworld divinities)— libations, prayers, and vows. A considerable number of altars of varying sizes was found in all regions of the Sanctuary. They include the early rock altars, one in the region of the Rotunda of Arsinoe, one later covered by the great Altar Court; altars of smaller dimensions and more typical forms, circular or rectangular, in clay, brick (Museum Cases B1 and B3), and stone of which, in most cases, only the foundations are preserved. They also included sacred hearths (*escharai*), for instance, in the Hall of Choral Dancers and the Hieron, and pits for libations to the underworld gods, round (in the Orthostate Structure beneath the Rotunda of Arsinoe) or square (outside the Rotunda and near its entrance).

At the great annual festival, processions probably moved from altar to altar on successive days. But actually we know very little about that festival. Even its date is unknown; it is a mere conjecture that it was celebrated late in July. If so, it may survive in the popular summer festival now celebrated in honor of Hagia Paraskevi at the spring in a plane tree grove of Palaiopolis on July 26. At least from the third century B.C. on, the Samothracians annually sent out invitations to these festivals throughout Greece and Asia Minor, and ambassadors (*theoroi*) from many cities and even from such organizations as the theater guild (Dionysiac *technitai*) of Teos participated along with ambassadors from the city of Samothrace, the local population, and other visitors. In some cases, such ambassadors were also delegated, *as Hieropoioi*, to offer sacrifices in Samothrace for the welfare of their states.

Early in the third century B.C., the great Rotunda of Arsinoe, at the entrance of which and in which sacrifices were performed, may have served the solemn gathering of these ambassadors. It is possible that the construction of this

Fig. 13. Fragmentary Parapet Block from the Rotunda of Arsinoe.
Early Third Century B.C.

spectacular building was connected with the organization of the international festival. Its decoration of bucranes and libation bowls refers to its use (Museum Hall A, Fig. 13).

During the celebration, a ritual drama representing a sacred marriage (*hieros gamos*) was performed, perhaps in the Hall of Choral Dancers built in the fourth century B.C. on the site of an old sacrificial area. By that time, it was believed that the search for the vanished maiden, which was undoubtedly followed by a celebration of her union with the underworld god, represented the wedding of Kadmos and Harmonia. It has been conjectured that the graceful frieze from the Hall of Choral Dancers (Museum Hall B, see Fig. 33) alludes to that wedding.

About 200 B.C., a theater was built in front of the Altar

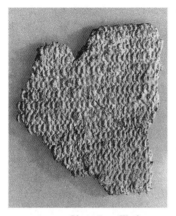

Fig. 14. Fragment of Chain Mail
Found in the Hall of Votive
Gifts. Hellenistic.

Fig. 15. Bronze Fishhook Dedicated as a Votive Gift.

Court and probably a Dionysiac competition was then added
to the public festival. Evidently it was here that local stories
were brought onto the stage. Early in the second century
B.C., the Samothracians honored a poet from Iasos in Caria,
author of the tragedy *Dardanos*, for this and other beneficial
actions toward the island, the town, and the Sanctuary.

The votive gifts dedicated in the Sanctuary covered the
wide range of works of art and objects of all kinds customary
in Greek places of worship: buildings and altars, statues of
bronze and marble (of which only fragments are preserved),
statuettes of marble and clay (Museum Case B4), armor
(Fig. 14), pieces for personal adornment, vases, and so on.
As the glory of the Sanctuary had its origin in the situation
of the island on an important sea-lane, its divinities became
special patrons of sailors. The Kabeiroi, identified by the
Greeks with the Dioskouroi, protectors and guides of sailors, became particularly popular for this reason. In fact, the
Sanctuary was filled with the votive gifts of those saved from

dangers on the sea. The dedication of such humble objects as shells and fishhooks (Museum Cases B1 and C2, Fig. 15) is common in Samothrace and we possess an epigram by the great Hellenistic poet Kallimachos referring jokingly to the dedication of a saltcellar by a poor fellow whom the gods saved from the storms of debt. He may have seen such an object in the Sanctuary (Museum Case B1).

The mysteries of the Great Gods were renowned and revered in the Greek world as early as the fifth century B.C. Together with the mysteries of Eleusis, they stand out as the main examples of one aspect of the religious experience of ancient Greece which, later in antiquity, was to expand throughout the ancient world. While exclusive rites secretly performed by certain social groups were otherwise not uncommon in Greece, these mysteries were distinguished from public cults not only by their secrecy and limitation to certain participants, but also by a number of other characteristics.

Participation was not defined by distinctions of sex, age, or social status. It was a matter of individual free choice. While in Eleusis, it was racially limited to Greeks and socially to free people, in Samothrace, men, women, and children of all nations, slave and free alike, could obtain initiation.

This all-inclusive admission made the Samothracian mysteries more like a Christian community than any other phenomenon of Greek religion. It was, furthermore, enhanced by the fact that initiation was a matter quite apart from the annual festival and that individuals or groups could obtain it whenever they came to the gods and on any date of their choice, as the inscribed records show. While initiation could be obtained only in Samothrace, at least from the Hellenistic time on, groups of initiates organized themselves into religious clubs as Samothrakiasts and had their own congregational centers in numerous cities.

Though the rites included common religious practices

such as sacrifice and invocation, they were differentiated from them by the revelation of a sacred story —such as that of the rape of Persephone at Eleusis— and by the showing of meaningful symbols to the initiate. Some kind of reference to and interpretation of the legend, as well as some exhibition of the symbols, took place. In Samothrace, Herodotus tells us, the *mystes* learned to understand the deeper significance of the ithyphallic images of Hermes-Kadmilos and, centuries later, a man of the intellectual level of Varro claims that certain symbols shown in the Samothracian mysteries symbolized Heaven and Earth.

By such revelations and through a kind of communion with the gods, both of which were kept strictly secret, the *mystes* obtained assurance of certain privileges. In general, he hoped for good fortune and especially protection from perils at sea. A purple scarf given during the initiation and tied around the abdomen served as a magic charm to protect sailors and travellers from danger. It is probable that the Samothracian iron rings exposed to the "divine power" of the magnet stone were another such protective symbol obtained in the initiation (Fig. 9).

But it was not only material well-being in life that was secured by participation in the mysteries. In Eleusis, as early as the end of the seventh century B.C., the initiate was promised a happy afterlife. In Samothrace, such a promise is not documented. But a scene of heroes in the netherworld on an Archaic relief now in Paris and the fifth-century bust of Teiresias (Museum Hall B, see Fig. 56) point to the same idea. In later times, at least, it was also claimed that participation in the Samothracian mysteries made men morally better. The initiates often called themselves "pious".

One feature common to Eleusis and Samothrace is the existence of two degrees of initiation: *myesis* and *epopteia*. But while at Eleusis the obtaining of these two degrees, bound as it was to the annual festival, had to be separated by

Photo Anna Wachsmann

Fig. 16. Marble Lamp. Archaic.

at least a year's interval, in Samothrace the higher degree of *epopteia* could be obtained immediately after the *myesis*, even on the same day. Again, while at Eleusis the *epopteia* seems to have been obligatory to complete the rites, the records of initiations here show that initiation into the higher degree was an exception rather than the rule. This implies that conditions were attached to it which made many people shy from obtaining the higher degree. As the social status of mere *mystai* and, on the other hand, of *mystai* who were also *epoptai* shows, these conditions were not of a social or financial character. It seems probable that a moral requirement was involved and that a hearing in which the applicant had to confess whatever "sins" he had committed, a documented feature of the Samothracian mysteries unique in Greek religion, may have preceded the *epopteia* (see p. 81).

As at Eleusis and elsewhere, the initiation ceremonies evidently took place at night by the light of torches and lamps. Torches appear repeatedly on Samothracian monuments (Museum Case B1 and stele drawn by Cyriacus of Ancona

Fig. 17. Black-Glazed Terracotta Lamp.
Archaic.

in Hall B, see Fig. 7), and stones perforated to support huge torches were found in various places in the excavations. Marble lamps dating from the seventh through the fourth centuries were also found (Museum Case C6, Fig. 16). Made not to be suspended but to be carried or to stand on a support, they evidently were used in the nocturnal rites. But the profusion of clay lamps recently discovered (Fig. 17), some of them incised with the magical initial of the Great Gods Θ, others stamped with a monogram ΘΕ having the same meaning, the latter evidently manufactured for exclusive use in the Samothracian cult, suggests that at some point in the ceremonies every initiate carried a lamp.

The excavations have also furnished ample evidence of banqueting in the Sanctuary. This may not have been of "sacramental" character or part of the secret rites. But it, as well as purification, may have preceded or followed the actual secret initiation. It is probably rooted in sacrifices, including the killing of victims and pouring of libations, after which the participants feasted and drank. A deposit of ceramics, including both fine Greek ware and native handmade pots dating as early as the seventh century B.C., (Museum Cases C1 and C3, see Figs. 3, 62) was found beneath the later Hall of Choral Dancers together with remnants of sacrificial meals and gigantic kantharoi. Drinking of wine to the degree of intoxication therefore seems to have been a very early custom in the Samothracian rites. Later, too, the prevailing form of drinking vessel remains the kantharos (Fig.

Photo Anna Wachsmann
Fig. 18. Black-Glazed Kantharos.
Fourth Century B.C.

18), often incised with the magical initial of the Gods. But kylikes were also used (Museum Case C4). In the Hellenistic period, simple conical bowls having a Θ incised in the center before firing are common. Smaller shallow bowls and dishes, including fish plates (Museum Cases C4 and C6), were evidently used for modest portions of food. Every initiate seems thus to have been provided with a cup, a bowl, and a lamp. From the fifth century through the Hellenistic age, many fragmentary bowls and plates occur which bear graffiti, mostly single letters, that sometimes were later scratched out (Museum Case C11). These letters seem to mark the vessels as sacred property of the Gods to be used by the initiates in the mysteries. In the Roman period, glass was commonly used for such vessels.

As in other mysteries, the initiates certainly wore crowns. A Hellenistic terracotta head of a woman wearing a heavy garland under a veil (Museum Case B1) may be taken to be the representation of a *mystis* (Fig. 19).

All these details are suggestive of the atmosphere that prevailed in the mysteries. A

Photo Anna Wachsmann
Fig. 19. Head of a Terracotta Statuette Representing an Initiate. Hellenistic.

41

Drawn by Stuart M. Shaw
Fig. 20. Tentative Reconstruction of the Interior of the Anaktoron.

more precise idea of the succession of ceremonies may be obtained from the two major buildings that served for the performance of the essential rites of initiation.

Preparations for the initiation probably took place in a small room, a kind of vestry to the south of the Anaktoron which has been called the Sacristy. Here there were benches and here, too, it seems that the novice received a lamp and may have been vested in white garments.

The *myesis* took place in the Anaktoron, the "House of the Lords" (Fig. 20, see Figs. 11, 22, 24-26). A large hall accessible through three doors, it offered space for a considerable crowd. Most of those who witnessed the ceremonies, probably former initiates, were gathered in the southern part of the building and stood or sat on wooden benches placed on an ascending floor so that they might see what happened in the center of the hall. A grandstand built on wooden scaffolding along most of the eastern and northern sides of the building offered "boxes" for a privileged group of witnesses. The initiates were probably led in through the wide main door. Some action took place in the southeastern corner; originally it seems to have been a mere lustration rite at a basin. At a later period, the initiate stepped onto a narrow threshold and probably poured a libation over a sacred stone at the bottom of a round pit. That pit was ordinarily covered by a removable wooden lid. Probably at the final moment of the *myesis*, the initiate was placed and presumably seated on a circular wooden platform opposite the main door and ritual dances were performed around him. After the *myesis*, he was led to the northern chamber. He stepped up to one of the two doors that gave access to it and in this inner sanctum he must have performed some ritual action and been shown some sacred symbols —probably those which Varro interpreted as meaning Heaven and Earth. At no time was anyone allowed to enter this sanctum before he was initiated.

It seems likely that the *mystes* then returned to the Sacristy and here received some document certifying his initiation. On the walls of the building, at least in later times, he could see many inserted marble slabs commemorating former initiations by name and date and, if he paid for it, he could himself order his name to be so inscribed.

Only after he had thus become a pious *mystes* could he proceed, if he wished, to acquire the higher degree, the *epopteia*, in the building specifically called the Sanctuary or Hieron (TO IEPON, see Figs. 34, 35), in the southern part of the sacred precinct. Its façade, completed in the late Hellenistic period and offering a temple-like aspect, was lighted by huge torches. None but the fully initiated could ever enter the building. But even the initiate who sought *epopteia* seems to have had to undergo a preliminary out-of-door ceremony at the side of the Hieron and close to its entrance (see p. 81). Here, two marble stepping stones, each just large

Fig. 21. Torch Stone Flanked by Stepping Stones outside the Hieron.

enough for a person to stand on, flanked another great lighted torch (Fig. 21). It seems likely that the aspirant stood on one stone, while a priest, interrogator, or witness stepped onto the other and that the future *epoptes* had thus to confess major sins and obtain purification from guilt, if such was obtainable. Meanwhile, inside the building, spectators had assembled, naturally formerly initiated *epoptai*, who sat on benches along the side walls. The *mystes* seems to have been led into the interior through the main door. Near the entrance, purification and lustration rites were probably performed. There followed a sacrifice on a sacred hearth in the center of the cella.

The *epoptes* was then probably seated in the rear part of the building, there to see with his own eyes a revelation, as the term *epopteia* indicates. Here, the hierophant entered into the apse and emerged to stand on a special stone (*bema*), reciting a liturgy and showing symbols while, at intervals, he seems to have performed invisible rites, including the pouring of libations to the underworld gods, behind the curtains that separated the apse from the hall in which the spectators were seated.

When the interior of the Hieron was revised, *ca.* A.D. 200, the main door was widened and, ultimately, in the Constantinian period, the threshold was cut down to allow the entrance of sacrificial animals into the building. In connection with these changes, parapets were built to protect the spectators and a crypt was installed in the apse, while a hole in the bema, ordinarily covered by a wooden lid, now allowed the traditional libation to be poured onto the rock beneath it. These alterations served the Kriobolia and Taurobolia of Magna Mater, an Anatolian divinity not essentially different from the Samothracian Axieros, which were added to the *epopteia* in late antiquity. In these rites, the initiate or a priest on his behalf descended into a pit —here the lower level of the apse— and the blood of sacrificed animals was poured over him from above in a kind of baptismal rite.

This seems to be all that can now be stated about the Great Gods of Samothrace, their rites and mysteries, on the basis of the written documents and the excavations. The essential content of legend, creed, and experience will forever remain unknown to all those not initiated. Yet the visitor to the conspicuous ruins of the Sanctuary, seeing them in the framework of a savage and grandiose mountain landscape comparable with, if different from, that of Delphi, may recapture that awe of the immortal forces of nature which here, as there, impelled people to worship the gods.

III

The Excavations

History of the Excavations

In 1863, M. Champoiseau, a French consul then stationed at Adrianople, impressed with the ruins of the Sanctuary, began excavations that led by chance to the discovery of the Nike of Samothrace. The remnants of the figure were shipped to Paris together with some other marbles. Stimulated by these discoveries, the French government sent to the island MM. Deville and Coquart who, in 1866, mapped the then visible ruins and made trial excavations in several places. Again, some architectural pieces and inscriptions were transported to the Louvre. In 1873 and 1875, two Austrian expeditions directed by A. Conze made extensive excavations. They uncovered the Propylon of Ptolemy II and the Stoa and made partial excavations in the Hieron, the Hall of Choral Dancers, and the Rotunda of Arsinoe. The results of their work were made known in two big volumes which were, for their time, a magnificent publication. By agreement with the Turkish government, the Austrians partitioned their finds. Numerous architectural blocks, some ornamental pieces sawed off such blocks, and sculptures were taken to the Kunsthistorisches Museum in Vienna. Others, destined for the Turkish government, were shipped to Gallipoli, but only a few of them, chiefly frieze blocks of the Propylon of Ptolemy II, reached the Museum in Istanbul. The rest seem to have disappeared. In 1891 Champoiseau returned to Samothrace and took the fragments of the ship on which the Nike stood to Paris. On that occasion, he discovered the Theater. From 1923 to 1927 MM. Salač and Chapouthier made partial excavations in various buildings of the Sanctuary.

In 1938, the Institute of Fine Arts of New York University began excavations in Samothrace which immediately led to the discovery of the Anaktoron. Trial excavations were also made in the town, and various ruins and cemeteries were located.

Since 1939, this expedition has concentrated on a systematic excavation of the major part of the Sanctuary, a task continued since 1948 after the interruption of the war. In 1954 incidental discoveries led to the excavation of a nekropolis on the construction site of the Xenia Hotel and to the opening of some tombs in another cemetery to the southeast of the Sanctuary. Since 1957, a large section of that cemetery has been excavated. In 1956, a part of the colonnaded façade of the Hieron was re-erected. Since 1962, excavations have fully investigated the Stoa, the Propylon of Ptolemy II and the Hall of Choral Dancers and revealed numerous buildings and other monuments on the Eastern and Western Hills of the Sanctuary (Fig. 22).

Itinerary

A path opposite the Museum's entrance leads to the gate in the fenced archaeological area. Modern paths and the present state of the remains are indicated on Plan III. Bold-face numbers in the text correspond to those on Plans III and IV.

Many visitors prefer first to inspect the major cult buildings in the center of the Sanctuary and then to proceed to its periphery, and this *Guide* follows that route.

Others prefer to follow the route of the ancient visitor from the Propylon of Ptolemy II (**26**), as outlined on p. 49.

To follow the former course, the visitor should proceed past the custodian's booth to a pair of stairways which allow him to cross the central torrent bed to the Anaktoron (**23**)

Fig. 22. Air View of the Sanctuary (1981).

and the Rotunda of Arsinoe (**20**). A path at the southeast of the latter leads to the Hall of Choral Dancers (**17**), from which he may proceed southward to the Hieron (**15**), the Hall of Votive Gifts (**16**), the Altar Court (**14**), and the Theater (**13**). From the southeast corner of the Hieron, he may follow a path that leads up the slope to the Southern Nekropolis (**27**) and then descends to cross the eastern torrent to the Propylon of Ptolemy II (**26**).

From this point, he may proceed on a path leading northeastward to the city wall and continue on to the fortress of the Gattilusi. From the site of these towers, he may look down on the lower town, its now sand-filled harbor, the mole of which is still recognizable in outline under the water, and near which he can see the contour of a large Early Christian church.

Turning to the right after recrossing the eastern torrent bed, he may follow a path that skirts the monuments of the Eastern Hill (**24-25**), and proceed along the ancient stepped ramp at west. Turning left on a path above the Rotunda of Arsinoe, he may continue south of the Hieron, to ascend to the monument once dominated by the Victory of Samothrace (**12**), whence he may view the entire Sanctuary save its easternmost part, and to the Stoa (**11**). From the northwest corner of that building he may proceed down to the lower terraces of the Western Hill (**1-12, 29**), at the east of which he can rejoin the path which, to the left, leads to the Museum, to the right to a series of dining rooms.

To follow the ancient route through the Sanctuary, the visitor should continue along the path from the entrance to the Theater, proceed south of the Altar Court and the Hieron and along the path to the Propylon of Ptolemy II (**26**), the ancient entrance to the Sanctuary. Turning to the right after recrossing the eastern torrent bed, he may follow a path that skirts the monuments of the Eastern Hill (**24-25**), and proceed along the ancient stepped ramp at west, which ends at the Rotunda of Arsinoe. Visiting in turn the Anaktoron (**23**), the Rotunda of Arsinoe (**20**), the Hall of Choral

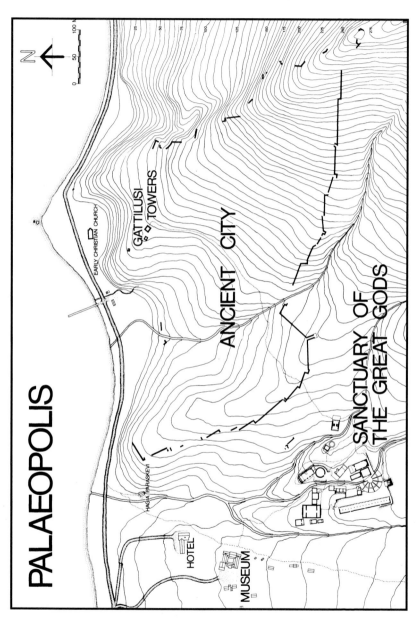

Fig. 22. Sketch Map of Palaiopolis

Drawn by John Kurtich

Dancers (**17**), the Hieron (**15**), the Hall of Votive Gifts (**16**), and the Altar Court (**14**), he may again ascend the slope east of the southeast corner of the Hieron and turn right on the path to the monument of the Victory of Samothrace (**12**) and the Stoa (**11**). From the northwest corner of the Stoa he may descend to the lower terraces of the Western Hill (**1-12, 29**).

Situation and Development of the Sanctuary

A massive mountain range crowned by the Peak of the Moon (Phengari) dominates the island. Detached from it, a lower craggy mountain now bearing the name of Hagios Georgios stretches from south to north to the east of the site and tapers to a low promontory at the beach. Its northern-most peak crowns the vast enceinte of the ancient town, serving as the acropolis, and its promontory forms the start-ing point of the mole once protecting the ancient harbor from northern and northeastern winds. On the other side, the city wall dating partly from the Archaic, partly from the Hellenistic age, runs down the steep mountainside, crosses a ravine, and encloses a lower western hill near the beach. At its foot, outside the ancient city, the small church of Hagia Paraskevi is situated (Fig. 23).

Here a small river falls into the sea between the western hill of the town and the lower hill on which the Hotel Xenia stands. This river is fed by two streams meeting at a point opposite the Museum and farther to the south a third stream falls into the eastern branch. The eastern and western of these three streams frame the Sanctuary of the Great Gods which covers an area of *ca.* 50,000 square meters on the two hills between them. There never was an enclosure around this large sacred area within which the Sanctuary gradually grew and expanded.

The promontory between the eastern and central streams contained the entire Sanctuary in its earlier phases. This hill drops almost vertically into the eastern ravine but slopes gently towards the central river. The main structures of the Sanctuary, including all those of early origin antedating the Classical period, are crowded together on this slope.

Around 650 B.C., when the Greeks had arrived, a nearby area on the site of the later Hall of Choral Dancers was used for sacrifice and banquets. But during the sixth century the area of worship expanded farther, including sacrificial places not only on the site of the Hall of Choral Dancers, but also at the very southern boundary of the later Sanctuary, in the location later used for the Altar Court. Around 550 B.C., the Hall of Votive Gifts was built to the north of that later structure facing the river. And an earlier apsidal Hieron beneath the later marble building probably formed part of the same building program to satisfy the demands of the mystery rites.

In the fifth century, the Hieron was renewed and probably provided with a sculptured marble pediment. At the same time, in the northern part of the Sanctuary, a Sacred Rock was provided with a pavement. On the Eastern Hill, the construction of a circular pavement, surrounded by steps for spectators, gave monumental form to an area at the entrance to the Sanctuary that may previously have served sacrificial purposes in its natural state. Early in the fourth century, a small but richly stuccoed building of still uncertain purpose was added, abutting the steps.

Also in the first half of the fourth century B.C., the Orthostate Structure was built on the site later occupied by the Rotunda of Arsinoe to serve for the *myesis*, a rite which in Archaic and earlier Classical times was performed in a still undiscovered location.

After the middle of the fourth century a great marble building, the Hall of Choral Dancers, was constructed; an Ionic porch facing northwest formed its entrance. This first marble structure in the Sanctuary initiated a new phase of monumental development. It was followed, between 340 and

330 B.C., by the great Altar Court which, like its Archaic neighbor, the Hall of Votive Gifts, faced the river to its west. Shortly afterwards the Hieron was renewed as a splendid marble building stretching behind both these structures, though its northern porch was only completed more than 175 years later. Above it, on the Eastern Hill of the Sanctuary, Arrhidaios and his co-ruler, Alexander IV, Alexander the Great's infant son, dedicated still another marble Doric building after the former's accession to the throne as Philip III. Erected between 323 and 317 B.C., it dominated the older paved circle in front of it and presumably took over not only the site but also the function of its stuccoed predecessor. To the north, on the western slope of the same hill, there was built a small Doric Rotunda, conceivably a cenotaph.

In the second half of the fourth century, too, the ridge to the west, between the central and westernmost streams, was included in the Sanctuary, which thus expanded once more. The earliest structure yet explored in this western area is a long, three-room building at the base of the slope, probably for ritual dining. Other fragmentary walls at the top of the ridge attest structures which may have served to shelter visitors in the same period.

In the years between 288 and 270, Queen Arsinoe dedicated her conspicuous Rotunda. The construction of the building forced relocation of the functions previously served by the Orthostate Structure northward to the site of the later Anaktoron, whose immediate predecessor was constructed at this time.

Between 285 and 281 B.C., Ptolemy II gave a new and monumental character to the entrance of the Sanctuary by the construction of a marble Propylon, spanning the eastern ravine, which formed the boundary of the sacred area on that side. Its eastern, Ionic façade received the road from the city walls, while its western, Corinthian porch led, by a steep, now destroyed ramp, both to the complex of structures on the Eastern Hill and, around them, past the building dedicated by Kings Philip and Alexander, to the paved way toward the central cult buildings.

In the course of the third century, other ambitious buildings and engineering projects, animated by that Hellenistic sense of setting so different from the earlier accumulation of individual units, radically changed the aspect which the Sanctuary presented to its visitors. Largest and earliest of these works was the construction of a huge Stoa on the crest of the western ridge, facing and overlooking the old shrines, precincts, and altars. To the north, on a lower terrace, a three-room marble building, entered by a colonnaded Ionic porch, probably an addition to the facilities for ritual dining in this area, was dedicated later in the century by an unknown woman from Miletus. South of it, an intermediate terrace supported another dining room and a long, enclosed hall for the display of a warship dedicated to the Great Gods, and west of it an even larger marble building was begun but never completed, all within the Hellenistic period. Finally, at the end of the century, the Theater was constructed opposite the Altar Court, beneath the southern end of the Stoa, and above the cavea, shortly afterward, there was installed the monument whose center was occupied by the Victory of Samothrace.

During its earlier development, the Sanctuary had been widely and loosely spread out over hill and dale with its individual elements on different levels, thus necessitating descending and ascending paths which crossed the stream and wound around to reach the entrances of the various older buildings. The spirit of the new age aimed at improving that situation and regularizing the surroundings of buildings both old and new. Retaining walls of boulders lined the river which once had formed the western boundary of the Sanctuary and now flowed through it from the Theater to the Rotunda and created a unified level among the older buildings on the east side and with the newly developed area on the west. A mighty, buttressed wall was raised against the western ridge to support the terrace in front of the northern part of the Stoa and, at the same time, to create more space at the foot of the ridge; neighboring areas were likewise regularized with retaining walls and filling.

The Sanctuary had, with these works, achieved the basic form that it was to retain to the end of antiquity. Except for the marble porch added to the Hieron at the middle of the second century and a series of three smaller treasury-like buildings added somewhat later along the western limits of the Sanctuary, building activity in later Hellenistic and Roman times was confined to the repair and revision of earlier structures, including the construction of the Anaktoron and the re-roofing of the Rotunda.

When the pagan cult was forced out of existence in the later fourth century after Christ, it was completely abandoned and for many centuries only decay and willful destruction prevailed. Part of the Roman walls regulating the river soon collapsed. In the fifth century of the Christian era, while most of the old buildings were still upright, lime burners built a huge kiln to the south of the Rotunda of Arsinoe in which they consumed marble spoils from the surroundings buildings and monuments. About the middle of the sixth century, a terrific earthquake caused the complete collapse of the already ruined buildings of the Sanctuary. Lime burners and stone robbers continued to exploit the ruins, and this practice persisted into recent times. Over the heaps of debris, nature spread a wild growth of shrubs and, along the river, of plane trees. Only here and there did parts of terraces and marble blocks emerge above the surface. In the tenth century, the Western Hill temporarily provided the site and the spoils to build an imposing Byzantine fort. It, too, was destroyed and overgrown in due time.

The central and earlier section of the Sanctuary has been systematically uncovered and much of the Eastern and Western Hills has been exposed. Excavation has been carried down to the bedrock wherever possible and laid bare whatever is preserved of the oldest strata beneath later structures. An unusually abundant quantity of marble blocks is preserved from the superstructures of the major buildings owing to the fact that after the Middle Ages Samothrace was for many centuries almost inaccessible and thus, save for local vandalism, protected from exploitation of its ruins for building purposes. So far as the difficulties of the terrain allowed, the excavators have tried to group these blocks on and around the site of individual structures or in their vicinity in order to allow the visitor to study their architectural features, an arrangement which is supplemented by partial restorations of some of the buildings in the Museum (Halls A and B). The major structures now visible in the excavation are briefly explained below in topographical order.

The Anaktoron (Figs. 11, 20, 22, 24-26) **[23]**

This building, unusually well preserved at the south and east, where its walls are still upright to a height of some 4 meters, was constructed in the early Imperial period, according to the ceramic finds from its foundation ditches. It was the latest and most complete of a succession of structures for initiation into the mysteries (*myesis*). The Anaktoron was erected on the northernmost point of the narrowing ridge which allowed for the construction of a major building. It there occupied nearly the same location as its immediate predecessor. Of the latter structure, built together with the Rotunda of Arsinoe or just after it, only the lowest part of its west foundation, an oblique line of boulders and fieldstones just west of the Anaktoron, is preserved for most of its 31-meter length as is part of its south foundation, the short,

Fig. 24. View of the Anaktoron with the City Wall in the Background.

again oblique line of boulders upon which the western section of the Anaktoron's south wall rests. The southern end of the Anaktoron also overlaps the northernmost part of its Classical forebear, the Orthostate Structure, of which the best preserved parts are visible beneath the Rotunda of Arsinoe (p. 70).

The Anaktoron is oriented northwest-southeast. The only approach to it was from the south, from a sloping and gradually narrowing terrace in front of it. It was deeply cut into the hillside, and the lower parts of its eastern and southern walls were not visible in antiquity. Along the former side, a strong terrace wall of boulders was built at a distance of 0.50 meters from the outer wall to protect it from humidity and the pressure of earth. Unfortunately, with the destruction of the ancient building, the upper part of the terrace wall slanted forward and caused parts of the eastern wall to buckle. The preserved part of the northwestern corner has also slanted out of position towards the river valley.

The walls are built of limestone laid in mortar in a polygonal scheme to form its two faces; the center was filled with rubble. Four piers project inward from each long wall. Built of ashlar masonry, they served to reduce the very wide span and to support pairs of heavy beams for the timber roof, which was covered with tiles and hipped at the short sides (a restoration of part of the edge of the roof is exhibited in Museum Hall A). The upper wall may or may not have had windows, and its exact height, probably between 6 and 8 meters, is unknown. White stucco covered both wall and piers, which enclosed a space 27 by 11.58 meters. The floor was of earth.

Three doors on the western façade, a larger one flanked by two smaller ones, give access to the interior from the western terrace (some steps in front of the center door and an outer terrace wall to protect the structure toward the riverbed are modern). In the central threshold, one may still

Fig. 25. View of the Anaktoron from the South (the Sacristy in the Right Foreground).

see one of the bronze pans in which the left leaf of the door pivoted.

The earth floor was higher in the section of the building north of the northern entrance door —as it still is in some parts. This section formed an inner sanctuary, into which people were allowed to enter only after initiation. A marble stele (Museum Hall A, Fig. 11) prohibiting entry into this rear sanctuary was found in fallen position in front of its entrance. The wall supporting this upper level, built of red porphyry blocks on a limestone foundation, was interrupted in its western half by two doors, a wider eastern and a narrower western one. Steps from the lower level of the main hall gave access to these doors. Behind this wall, a large square porphyry block with a hole for a vertical beam is *in situ*. Evidently, this cross wall supported a wooden partition, possibly decorated and lower than the roof which, not unlike the iconostasis of Christian churches, separated the northern sanctuary from the main hall. The doors leading into it from the hall were flanked by two bronze statues of the Kabeiroi, raising their hands.

In the main hall, several elements of the interior installation are still preserved. An oven-shaped structure in the southeastern corner, square on the outside and circular inside, has a threshold too narrow for entrance into it but wide enough for a person to stand on. The interior has a recess separating its upper from its lower part. During the excavation, a sacred stone was found on natural soil at the bottom of the deep circular pit (now filled with earth). Apparently a removable wooden lid was posed on the inner ledge of the pit into which libations were poured on the sacred stone in its depths.

Along the eastern and most of the northern walls of the main hall, a number of limestone bases are preserved with horizontal cuttings for the insertion of beams. They evidently supported a wooden grandstand around two sides of the hall.

In the center of the hall near the eastern wall and in front of the eastern grandstand, remnants of a wooden platform burned in the final collapse of the building were found. The platform was circular and had a diameter of 3.25 meters.

For the interpretation of these remains and the rites performed in the Anaktoron, see Chapter II.

In the Museum, the visitor may see the stele prohibiting the uninitiated from entering the northern chamber and the reconstruction of the roof (Hall A); antefixes of this roof and one of the bronze door pans (Cases B3 and B1); stucco from the face of the inner walls (Case C12).

The building was better preserved at the time of excavation than it is now; porphyry and other stones from the eastern half of the retaining wall supporting the higher chamber at the north, the entire western section of this wall including the foundation, the porphyry threshold of the southern door, and two of the grandstand supports were willfully destroyed during World War II; the southeast pier, also damaged, has been rebuilt to strengthen the wall.

Leaving the Anaktoron, turning left and mounting a partly reconstructed ancient stairway (to the right a small stone terrace wall constructed for another road along the northern periphery of the Rotunda is visible), the visitor passes the southwestern outer corner of the building and, turning again to his left, reaches the entrance of the Sacristy.

The Sacristy (Fig. 26) [22]

This small building *ca.* 7 meters square is attached to the eastern half of the south wall of the Anaktoron, which served as its northern wall (Fig. 26). The foundation and part of the upper walls are preserved to a height of *ca.* 2 meters above the ancient floor level. As in the Anaktoron, the eastern end of the building is embedded in the hillside. Remnants of the entrance are recognizable in the center of the western wall. A side door near the eastern end of the south wall provided only for access to a small area between the eastern periphery of the Rotunda of Arsinoe and the terrace walls to its east. Indeed, the southwestern corner of the Sacristy almost touches the Rotunda. Its walls are built of small limestone polygonal masonry. It had an earth floor, and marble benches stood along its walls. Marble slabs of various sizes recording initiations were inserted into its stuccoed walls. Its timber roof was covered with tiles.

The present structure, built against the Anaktoron whose location, with that of the Rotunda of Arsinoe, dictated its size and shape, probably also dates in the early Imperial period. It was extensively repaired in the early fourth century after Christ, to which period belongs the preserved eastern wall.

In the depths beneath the Sacristy, remnants of the Orthostate Structure were found, other fragments of which were uncovered beneath the Rotunda and the Anaktoron. Overlying it was a corner of a later building, which possibly served the Hellenistic predecessor of the Anaktoron in the same fashion as the Sacristy served the Anaktoron itself. Partly destroyed during World War II, these remains have been covered to preserve what is left.

For the function of the building, see Chapter II.

In the Museum, the visitor may see two marble bench supports found in the Sacristy and now reused for their original purpose in Hall C, a fragmentary stamped roof tile (Ἱερὰ Θεῶν) in Case B2, and a set of curious crude lamps dating from the early fourth century after Christ which was found standing on the floor of the building in Case C6.

The Rotunda of Arsinoe (Figs. 13, 26-30) [20]

The Rotunda, situated to the south of the Anaktoron, was dedicated to the Great Gods by Queen Arsinoe II either when she was still the wife of King Lysimachos (between 288 and 281 B.C.) or in the next decade, when she was married to her brother, Ptolemy II. It was intended for sacrificial purposes and solemn gatherings at the annual summer festival.

It is the largest closed round building known in Greek architecture. Its gigantic foundation of limestone blocks erected on the steeply descending bedrock is preserved and exposed to an enormous height, and the huge marbles of its superstructure which the earthquake caused to fall on and around it are very numerous. These blocks have been assembled on the foundation and in the vicinity of the building.

The outer diameter of the euthynteria, its lowest marble course at ground level, is 20.219 meters, and the foundation itself is *ca.* 2.5 meters wide. The superstructure was built of Thasian marble. On the eastern side marble blocks of the euthynteria which supported the superstructure are still in place. Over this level, three steps, a molded base with a beautiful anthemion decoration (a well-preserved piece lies near the eastern foundation), and a high orthostate and string-course supported a marble wall to a height of 7.42 meters. Although it was smoothly dressed on the outside, the inner face of its wall was built of decorative drafted-margin masonry above the dado. The wall was topped by a molded binding course decorated, both inside and outside, with anthemia and palmettes. Over it there followed a decorative gallery of pilasters (2.83 meters high), the lower parts of which are separated by a parapet decorated in each interval with a rosette between two bucranes. The entire building has a height of 12.65 meters. On the inside, this gallery is fashioned of Corinthian half-columns; the altars between them have alternating pairs of paterae and bucranes. Above the parapet, the spaces between the pilasters were filled by marble screens. On the exterior, the gallery supported a Doric entablature, the large size of which is scaled to the height of the entire building rather than to that of the pilasters. On the inside, an Ionic entablature ran over the Corinthian capitals.

The roof, which rose above a gutter decorated with rinceaux and lion's-head waterspouts and capped by palmette antefixes, was originally conical in shape, largely covered with scale-shaped tiles that decrease in size, rank by rank. After an earthquake in the early Imperial age, its timbers were altered and the roof was converted into an octagonal pyramid crowned by a hollow marble finial decorated in relief with laurel leaves. The nature of the ceiling is unknown; it is possible that the roof timbers were screened by a suspended coffered wooden dome.

The entrance was on the southern side of the building. Over the door, which very likely was flanked by a pair of huge torches, the monumental dedicatory inscription of Queen Arsinoe was carved on the architrave in two lines of large and beautiful lettering. The only complete block of this inscription now preserved lies on the southeastern foundation of the building.

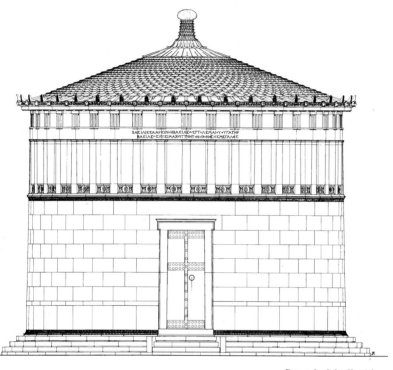

Fig. 27. Restored Elevation of the Rotunda of Arsinoe in the Hellenistic Period.

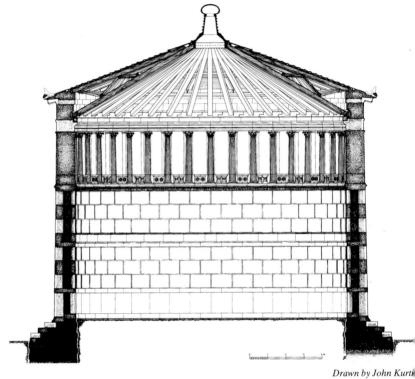

Drawn by John Kurti

Fig. 28. Restored Cross-section of the Rotunda of Arsinoe
in the Hellenistic Period.

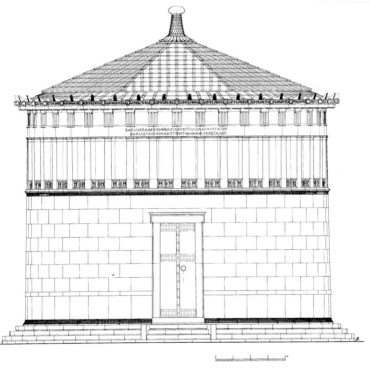

Fig. 29. Restored Elevation of the Rotunda of Arsinoe
in the Early Imperial Period.

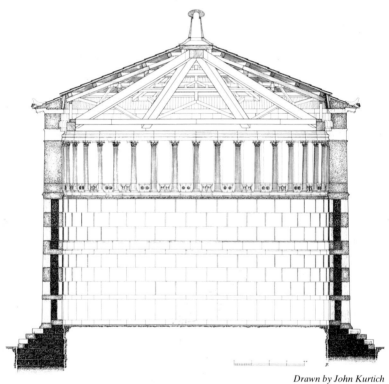

Fig. 30. Restored Cross-section of the Rotunda of Arsinoe
in the Early Imperial Period.

Outside the door, to the right of those who entered, a curious narrow, square shaft built against the foundation and contemporary with it goes deep down to the bedrock. It served for libations to the underworld gods. Foundations of two monuments or altars are situated to the east of it. The limestone foundation of another altar was found at the other side and at some distance from the door, to the southwest of the building. The interior of the Rotunda had an earth floor.

To protect the building from landslides, a terrace wall was built along its southeastern and eastern periphery and abutting the south wall of the Sacristy. An original piece of this terrace wall is preserved at the southern end only. It, too, is built of fieldstones and is posed on the lower part of an earlier rock retaining wall that continues toward the southeast. These retaining walls collapsed at least twice in antiquity; parts of them had to be renewed in the first century and perhaps in the third century after Christ. The latter section again fell shortly after World War II and has since been rebuilt.

For the function of the Rotunda, see Chapter II.

In the Museum, the visitor may see a partial restoration of the upper gallery and of the entablature, a fragment of the gutter, a large roof tile, and part of the crowning marble finial of the building (Hall A). Fragments of the dedicatory inscription are stored in the courtyard. Two fragmentary marble stelai showing a circular building with two torches flanking the door, seemingly a second-century descendant of the Rotunda that may have served as a branch Samothrakion in Kyzikos, are exhibited in Hall B. Many objects antedating the construction of the Rotunda of Arsinoe and important for the light they throw on the Samothracian cult as well as for the chronology of such objects were found in the huge quantity of earth fill in its interior and around its exterior. A selection of vases and lamps found in these fills is exhibited in Cases C4 and C6.

Even more marble blocks of the superstructure than are now preserved were originally found in the excavations. At least twenty large blocks were willfully destroyed, others disfigured by incised inscriptions, by Bulgarian soldiers during the Second World War.

Photo Anna Wachsmann
Fig. 31. View of the Orthostate Structure Beneath the Rotunda of Arsinoe.

Several ornamental blocks of the parapet, fragments of the sima, a lion's-head waterspout, and antefixes are preserved in the Ephesos-Museum in Vienna.

Excavation of the interior and the periphery of the Rotunda has shown that this whole area was previously used for the performance of sacrificial rites. In the depths, the excavators uncovered the larger part of an earlier structure:

The Orthostate Structure (Figs. 26, 31) **[21]**

Much of what is preserved of it is visible in the interior of the Rotunda of Arsinoe. But, while the structure apparently ended toward the south just beyond the later foundation of the Rotunda, it extended northward beneath the Sacristy (where its remains are now covered by earth) and the southernmost part of the Anaktoron. It measured 30.5 meters from north to south and 12 meters from east to west.

Oriented almost exactly north-south, the structure was

divided into a square central section and smaller northern and southern sections by cross walls, one now buried between the Rotunda and the Anaktoron, the other near the central east-west axis of the Rotunda. The outer walls and inner cross walls have fieldstone foundations, upon which a wall of yellow tufa was posed. This wall, parts of which are preserved over almost the entire southern cross wall and on the eastern wall, consisted of lower slabs, orthostates, and cover slabs. The space between the orthostates is divided into sections by transversely placed blocks and filled with fieldstones. The superstructure of the walls may have been of mudbrick. Whether they supported a roof to form a closed building or simply described an open precinct cannot now be determined from the evidence at hand. Pottery from the construction fillings dates the structure in the first half of the fourth century B.C., probably near the middle of that period.

Along the eastern side of the central and southern divisions, possibly once in the northern division as well, runs a low terrace, 2.5 meters wide, retained by a wall of large fieldstones. In connection with the Orthostate Structure, this terrace apparently functioned as a raised platform to accommodate those who attended the ceremonies performed in the main part of the building, analogous, therefore, to the wooden benches or grandstand found in a similar location in the Roman Anaktoron. To the west of the terrace, in the southern section of the Orthostate Structure, the excavators uncovered evidence for one ceremony, a sacrificial pit, remnants of which are still visible. Its top was level with the floor and beneath that level it was built of clay and small stones like a narrow circular oven. On its northern side a shaft, probably framed by boards, descended to a "sacred stone", a piece of marble upon which liquids were poured.

The fieldstone terrace wall appears to be the remnant of an older, higher structure, of which the original height is indicated by a fragment south of the Rotunda. It created a level terrace at about the level of the euthynteria of the Rotunda, apparently to support some structure, possibly the predecessor of the Orthostate Structure.

For the interpretation of these ruins, see Chapter II.

One may reach the lower area, outside the base of the Rotunda, by following the path southward, crossing the Hall of Choral Dancers (17), and returning northward along the modern river wall to the foundation of the Rotunda. At the foot of this foundation, the southwestern outer corner of the Orthostate Structure, built of huge blocks, is visible beneath the Rotunda. To the west of this corner is a sacred rock.

The Sacred Rock [19]

This is a high outcropping of blue-green porphyry. A smaller rock of the same variety, flattened on the surface, lies at its northeastern side. A fine pavement of the Classical period, made of the same yellow tufa used in the Orthostate Structure, spread to the northeast and northwest of this flattened rock and was separated from it by a narrow open channel. Standing on this pavement, a person evidently poured libations on the rock altar in front of this sacred rock, and the liquid flowed off from its surface into the channel.

On the other side of this area and at the foot of the high northwestern foundation of the Hall of Choral Dancers, there is a remnant of a statue base built of local red porphyry. Originally longer than it is today, its oblong shape suggests that it may have supported an equestrian figure.

The Hall of Choral Dancers (Figs. 32, 33, 55, 58) [**17**]

Situated in the very heart of the Sanctuary, opposite the processional road leading from the Eastern Hill, it was a Thasian marble building some 34 meters long and 20.7 meters wide (23 meters at the façade) —the largest and earliest of the Sanctuary's marble buildings. At the north (actually northwest; for simplicity the building is described as if it was orientated to the cardinal points) a deep, columnar porch or propylon gave access to the two sides of the closed building behind it.

Its limestone foundations were built largely of materials reused from yet unidentified earlier structures; the grey limestone used in the eastern part of the doorwall's foundation and in the short preserved portion of that of the median wall bonded to it may be the only newly-quarried stone. The eastern long side and southern end stood on bedrock, but the western side and especially the porch stood on often massive subfoundations of roughly polygonal, fieldstone boulders. Much of the south foundation, nearly all that of the median wall, and parts of those of the doorwall and of the façade were destroyed by a post-antique road and by a torrent which, following the line of the road, scoured the site.

The propylon was an elegant Ionic structure. Many of its blocks have been assembled on or adjacent to the building. Its colonnaded façade consisted of a central section flanked by two projecting wings.

A euthynteria and three profiled steps supported the Ionic colonnade which was distinguished by finely carved capitals with a bolster pattern above a singular drum at the top of each monolithic shaft. The latter is composed of flame palmettes, alternately upright and pendant, linked by extensions of their own tendrils to form bold, curvilinear frames (Museum Hall B; see Fig. 55). The entablature, consisting of

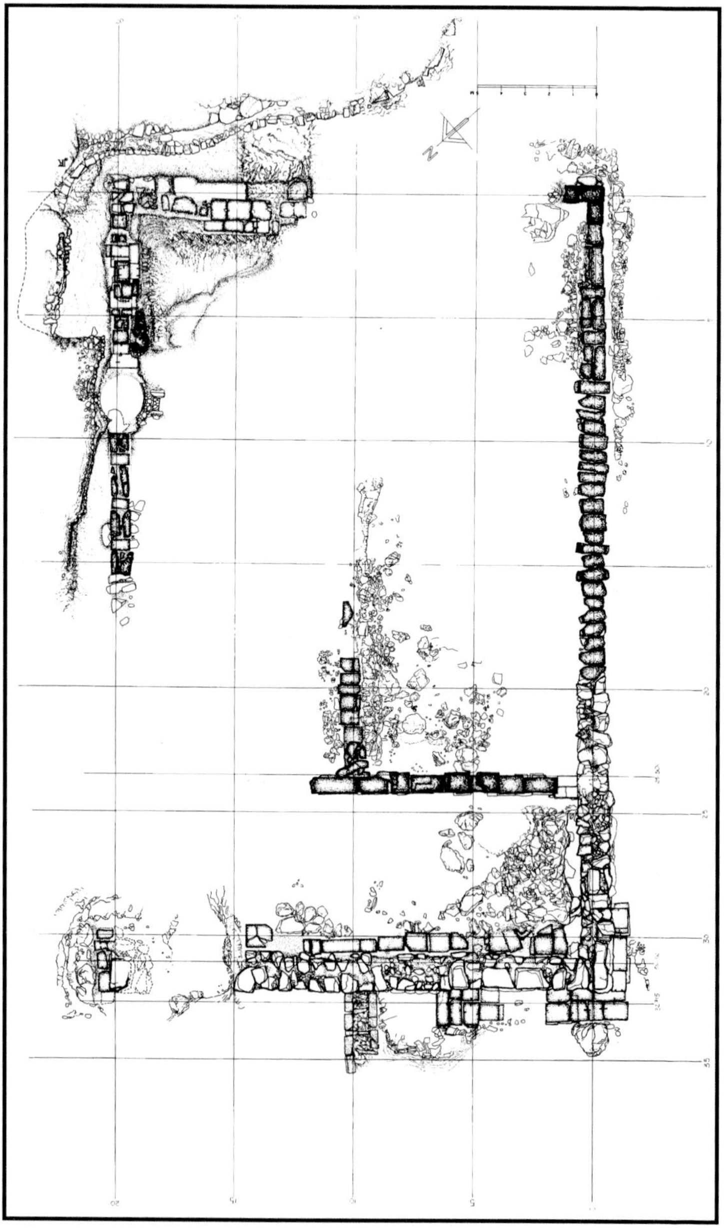

Fig. 32. Extant plan of the Hall of Choral Dancers *ca.* 340 B.C.

a triple-banded architrave, a frieze, dentils, and a cornice-gutter (geison-sima) carved in one block (several blocks of this category lie on the building), appears to be the earliest known example of a scheme destined to become standard in later Ionic and Corinthian architecture, combining the sculptured frieze and banded architrave of mainland Greece with the dentils characteristic of the frieze-less Ionic order of Asia Minor. The horizontal gutters were decorated with sculptured rinceaux, including flowers, buds, and spiral tendrils, and lion's-head waterspouts but, over the pediments of the wings, the raking gutters were simply painted. The greater part of the frieze beneath it was occupied by a chorus of dancers. Musicians, including a citharist, a tympanum player, and a flutist are interspersed among them (Museum Hall B; Fig. 33). Again, this frieze appears to be the earliest example of the extensive use of archaistic style in Greek sculpture, a style in which the features, proportions, and gait of the figures betray their late date, while the stylized folds of their garments and their swallow-tailed mantles allude to the remote past in the customary fashion of archaizing figures. In this case, it seems to allude to ritual dances performed on this very site. Like the rest of the entablature, the frieze encircled the whole building. The figures move in two directions, beginning at the building's southwest corner and proceeding toward the center of the façade where they must have approached some group or scene of which we now have no trace. Conceivably, it represented the legendary wedding of Kadmos and Harmonia, a ritual drama which was performed at the annual festivals.

There is evidence that sculptured reliefs occupied the pediments and that the latter were crowned by akroteria. Beneath them, the marble ceiling of the propylon was adorned with coffers of three sizes with separately worked carved lids. The extant lids all belong to the smallest size and were decorated with carved, doubtless originally painted, heads

Fig. 33. Detail of the Frieze from the Hall

seen in profile, full-face, and three-quarter views, which appear to have represented the various divinities, legendary figures, and heroic initiates honored in the Sanctuary. One of them (see Fig. 58), bears striking similarity to the style of Skopas, and recalls the fact that he made a renowned group of Aphrodite and Pothos for Samothrace (see p. 31) that may have stood within this very structure. Indeed, Skopas seems to have been the designing architect-sculptor of this building.

To allow access to its porch, the ground level to the north of the Hall of Choral Dancers was raised with an enormous earth filling, covering earlier monuments. To support it, a strong wall of fieldstones was built to the west of the building along the riverbed. Early in the Roman period, it was faced and reinforced by a concrete wall, which also regulated the stream and led it through a culvert. Fragments of

of Choral Dancers *ca.* 340 B.C.

the corresponding western concrete retaining wall, which likewise replaced an earlier fieldstone wall, may also be seen across the riverbed.

Behind the porch, the building was enclosed by marble walls in which courses of binders alternated with pairs of courses of stretchers; the latter were backed in limestone, and the inner surface of the walls were stuccoed. The inner floor of the western aisle was paved with marble and in it there were a sacred hearth (*eschara*), probably for sacrifices to the hero-founder of the cult, and a *bothros* or pit for libations to the gods. The eastern aisle had a slightly higher floor paved with a marble-chip mosaic. A door may have given access to the Hieron and the other structures in the southern part of the Sanctuary.

The pottery found in the excavations and the style of the porch show that the Hall of Choral Dancers was built *ca.* 340

B.C., very likely as a donation of Philip II of Macedon. But the site had a long earlier history as a sacrificial area. Such an area —the earliest in the Sanctuary— was discovered in the northwestern part of the Hall of Choral Dancers. It contained a dense accumulation of burned debris from sacrificial meals near a hearth built of rocks (traces visible in front of the center of the northwestern wall) as well as quantities of seventh-century pottery (see Figs. 3, 62).

The foundation of the doorwall of the Hall of Choral Dancers incorporates, in its western part, a remnant of an Archaic or Classical predecessor, to which a marble-framed *bothros* and a limestone *eschara* found by the Austrian excavators below the marble floor of the Hall of Choral Dancers evidently belonged. Like their fourth-century successors, these earlier *bothros* and *eschara* were located in the western part of the site.

For the religious significance of this area see Chapter II.

In the Museum, Hall B, sections of the frieze and an almost complete Ionic column as well as a fragmentary second capital and drum of the Propylon may be seen. Pieces of the sculptured coffered ceiling are exhibited in Case B4. In the center of Hall C, a finely decorated marble bench support stands on a base which was found in this area. A selection of handmade native and fine Greek subgeometric vases from the first half of the seventh century B.C. found in the early deposit occupies part of Case C1 and most of Case C3.

The geison-sima block from the southwest corner, a lion's-head waterspout, antefixes, fragments of the frieze and of the coffers are in the Ephesos-Museum in Vienna.

This description of the ruin and its history includes evidence obtained in the Austrian excavations which had been destroyed before the American work began.

The southwest corner of the Hall of Choral Dancers is very close to the northeast corner of the Hieron.

The Hieron (Figs. 34, 35, 53, 60) **[15]**

This structure, bigger than the Anaktoron and in its Doric splendor competing with the Rotunda of Arsinoe, dominates the background of the old Sanctuary. Its imposing ruins were always partly visible in the dense overgrowth that covered the site until the recent excavations and were attributed by Cyriacus of Ancona to a temple of Poseidon —an allusion to Homer, who made Samothrace a seat of the sea god. Now the ruin is visible in its totality, and five of its columns have been reconstructed to give the visitor an idea of the building's original grandeur. Approximately 800 marble blocks of its superstructure were found and today stand partly on the foundation, partly around it, the greatest number to the south.

In its present form, the building was begun early in the Hellenistic age, *ca.* 325 B.C. It was used for initiation into the higher degree of the mysteries, the *epopteia*. Officially it was called The Sanctuary, TO IEPON. But the original project was not fully executed at the time and the colonnaded façade with its sculptured pediment as well as the crowning elements of the roof were only added about 175 years later. It underwent several restorations, the major one in the early Imperial age.

The long, narrow structure, oriented approximately north-south, measures almost 40 meters from its northern façade to its apsidal end and has a width of *ca.* 13 meters. The façade faced an open triangular area in which traces of a large rectangular altar, originally dating from the Archaic period, and of a covered Roman drain are visible. To the south, an imposing polygonal terrace wall of crystalline porphyry that marks the southern boundary of the Sanctuary is contemporary with the early Hellenistic building. In this terrace wall, opposite the southeastern corner of the building, a curious boss marked with a cross appears. The interval between the

Fig. 34. View of the Hieron from the Northwest.

Hieron and the terrace wall served as a road which led eastward towards the Propylon of Ptolemy II and, to the west, ascended a now partly preserved stairway opposite the southwestern corner of the building to give access to the upper part of the Theater. To the west, the Hieron is separated by narrow lanes from the Hall of Votive Gifts and the Altar Court. To the east, the hillside ascended toward the South Nekropolis and the entrance to the Sanctuary.

On this eastern side and close to the foundation, near the line of the entrance to the cella and now enclosed by a protective covering (Fig. 21), a large square block with a vertical hole probably served to support a huge torch. To the north and south of it, two stepping stones had lain since early times. The original form of the weathered southern marble block is visible. The corresponding northern block is covered by a higher and later stone, which nonetheless still lies beneath the level of the Hellenistic period. When the present Hieron was built, it, in turn, was overlaid with a third higher stone and a framework of vertical roof tiles was placed around the stepping stones. It is assumed that here, by torchlight, a preliminary hearing and confession took place before the *epopteia*.

A fragment of one of two more such torch supports originally flanking the façade of the building may be seen near its northwestern corner.

The foundation, solidly built of the same limestone used for the Rotunda of Arsinoe, is completely preserved and on its upper edge along the entire southern and much of the western and eastern sides, one sees still *in situ* the marble euthynteria. The material used is Thasian marble. On these three sides, a course with the profile of a step (toichobate) supported the marble walls. The marble wall was built of two high courses in alternation with one low binder of drafted-margin masonry above a smooth dado and string course, the thin high courses being backed by limestone. At the rear

corners, it terminated in pilasters. At the façade, the foundation is wider and here two additional steps were added beneath the entire porch. The porch resting on these steps consisted of two rows of six columns separated by two additional columns, one on each side in line with the projecting anta walls. The entire building was crowned by a Doric entablature topped by a beautifully carved rinceau gutter with lion's-head waterspouts and palmette antefixes. The raking sima was decorated with a pattern of alternating palmettes, lotus flowers and blossoms. Both pediments contained sculptures (the front in the round, the rear in relief) and were crowned by sculptured akroteria: a floral acanthus akroterion at each center (see Fig. 53) flanked by a Victory on each corner (see Fig. 60). The roof was tiled. The marble stylobate of the pronaos with traces where the four columns were placed is preserved. In front of it, the porch was paved in marble supported by a still preserved foundation of limestone rails running north-south, the intervals of which are filled with a stone packing.

The pronaos had an earth fill which may have been covered by a signinum floor. The inner eastern and western sides of the pronaos foundation show traces of the interruption of the building project. One can clearly see that the entire northern foundation of the pronaos as well as the northern portions of its lateral foundations were later attached or hooked into the originally executed parts. The jambs and lintel of the door were ornamented with a meander pattern (the extant fragments date from about A.D. 200, when the door was widened). Near the door an inscribed stele prohibited the uninitiated from entering the building. The lateral ends of the marble threshold have been placed in approximately their original position and show late cuttings for a ramp to facilitate the introduction of sacrificial animals into the interior.

In the pronaos, the visitor will notice several partially

preserved, marble beams from its ceiling. They supported marble coffers, the lids of which were decorated with sculptured reliefs, including figures of prancing centaurs.

On the interior (Fig. 35), the walls were stuccoed to imitate their exterior drafting. The dado was painted black, the wall largely red, then white and, at the top, it was decorated with moldings and an engaged Doric order in white stucco. A trussed roof with a clear span of 10.72 meters and a coffered, wooden ceiling beneath it, covered the hall. Bronze moldings adorned its coffers. Only the limestone underpavement of the floor is preserved throughout most of the interior. Originally it supported a marble floor which was still intact near the entrance at the time of the Austrian excavations. It showed traces of a grille near the entrance to regulate access into the interior. Along the side walls transverse limestone rails supported marble benches. The parapets that separate the center aisle from the seats of the spectators date from the revision of ca. A.D. 200. The western one contains marble spoils from a later restoration. Numerous fragments of Hellenistic marble bench supports in the form of lion's legs were found in the excavations. In the later restoration, some of the benches were renewed in similar form while others were replaced by massive marble seats. Several of these late replacements are now visible in both aisles. In the northwestern corner, there was a drain for liquid which flowed off to a marble spout on the outside. In the center of the forepart of the nave, the burned limestone frame of a small, square sacred hearth (*eschara*) sunk into the floor is preserved.

Two lateral doors (thresholds in the marble field to the south) gave access to this region of the cella and were probably used for the entry of spectators (previous *epoptai*).

The building is distinguished on the interior by an apse, part of the limestone wall of which is preserved. It is included in the rectangular cella, and the spandrels at the

Fig. 35. Restored Perspective of the Interior of the Hieron. *ca.* 325 B.C.

Drawn by Martin R. Jones

corners were probably filled with a stone packing. Its wooden roof, a section of a cone, was tent-like in shape. Around the apse, a "choir" section rises two steps above the floor (here the upper marble pavement is largely preserved though in the badly repaired form of the late restoration). In front of the apse, a large marble block was hollowed out, in this Roman revision, by a half-oval hole which has a ledge to support a removable wooden lid. Beneath this hole, which was undoubtedly used for pouring libations, the red porphyry rock upon which the building is placed emerges to the highest point in this area. It descends steeply towards a hollow framed by the center of the apse whose floor, however, was originally at the same level as the floor of the cella. In the Roman restoration, a crypt, accessible by wooden steps, was installed in the apse.

In the depths of the apse, one distinguishes the curved foundations of two apsidal forerunners of the Hellenistic building. One of these foundations, of regular limestone blocks, forms the footing of the present apse and appears to date from the fifth century B.C. The other, contained within it and built of irregular fieldstones, is attributed to the Archaic period.

For interpretation of the function of the building, see Chapter II.

Five columns and the center blocks of the architrave were re-erected in 1956, mainly from preserved ancient pieces. The steps beneath them are modern, inasmuch as none of the ancient blocks had escaped the stone robbers and lime burners. The work was sponsored by the Bollingen Foundation. The capital replaced in its original position on the corner column was returned to Greece by the Kunsthistorisches Museum in Vienna in an exchange of antiquities.

In the Museum, the visitor may see a partial restoration of the Doric entablature; a major part and many fragments of the southern floral akroterion; a plaster reconstruction of this akroterion; a fragment of the raking sima of the pediment and the inscribed stele from the entrance (Hall A); the akroterial Victory from the southwestern corner in Hall C and two fragments of hands from the comparable northwestern figure in Case C6; a fragmentary left corner figure from the pediment in Hall C and additional fragments of these pedimental sculptures and sculptured coffer lids in Case B4; fragments of terracotta antefixes from the ridge pole of the roof in Case B3; bronze ornaments from the doors and ceiling in Case C2; a fragment of a big marble candelabrum in torch form entwined by a snake in Case B1. Four lion's-head waterspouts are stored in the courtyard.

A number of architectural pieces from the superstructure, most of the statues of the northern pediment, and fragments from the southern pediment, a floral akroterion, and an akroterial Victory are now in the Ephesos-Museum in Vienna. The two latter sculptures replaced the Hellenistic pieces in the Samothrace Museum in the restoration of the early Imperial age that followed damage to the building by an earthquake.

This description of the ruin and its history includes evidence obtained in the Austrian excavations which had been destroyed before the American work began.

To the west of the northern part of the Hieron is the ruin of the Hall of Votive Gifts.

The Hall of Votive Gifts (Fig. 36) [16]

The major part of the rock foundation and the southern half of the underpavement of the floor are preserved. Only the northwestern corner was totally destroyed by erosion from the river flowing beneath it and has been completed in outline after the excavation.

The building forms a rectangle oriented north-south, having a length of 22.60 meters and a width of 10.70 meters. Its façade, looking west, was preceded by an outer step, a section of which is still preserved along the southern part of the western foundation. Of the superstructure, built in a fine, easily sawed imported limestone, only a few blocks (stereobate) are preserved above the southern end of the western foundation. The northern most of these blocks bears

86

a cutting for a wooden anta. The façade had an open Doric limestone colonnade between two such antae. The walls were curiously built of blocks of various sizes which decreased above to the size of small brick-shaped stones while wooden horizontal and vertical ties bound the masonry together. The entablature was partly of wood and limestone and supported a timber saddle roof with the considerable span of about 8 meters. Along the edge of the roof there ran a strongly projecting and finely carved stone cornice to which a ter-racotta gutter was nailed. The building was stuccoed on both the outside and the inside. It was built in this form about 540 B.C. to protect and exhibit votive gifts. It continued in use in the same form, with only minor restorations, for almost a thousand years. The small stone underpavement preserved in most of the interior dates from about 400 B.C.; beneath it were found many votive gifts of the preceding 150 years. Originally it probably supported a pebble mosaic floor with an outer border. From the Hellenistic period on, this pave-ment was covered by coats of stucco, several times renewed, of which patches of red and light green were preserved at the time of excavation.

The limestone foundation of a square monument is par-tially preserved outside and against the eastern end of the northern wall. It may have supported a Ptolemaic dedication, a colossal statue, of which the fragmentary base in Egyptian rose granite was found and lies fallen on the slope to the northwest.

For the purpose of the building, see Chapter II.

In the Museum, there are on exhibition some finely worked wall stones and cornices (Hall A); stucco fragments from the wall and a marble tool to smooth stucco, which was found on the floor broken and abandoned by a workman at the end of the pagan cult (Case C12, see Fig. 72); two gilded bronze letters from an inscrip-tion of the early Roman age, which were applied to the stuccoed architrave of the façade (Case C2); and votive gifts found beneath and upon the floor (Cases B1, C2, C4, C8, C11).

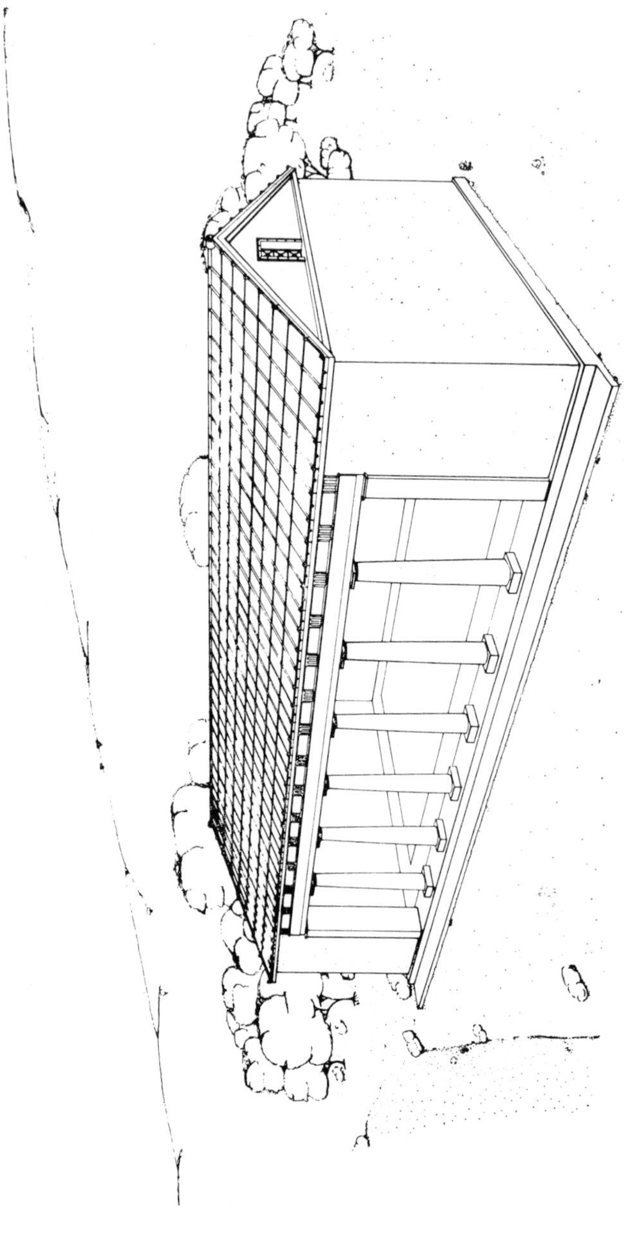

Fig. 36. The Hall of Votive Gifts. Restored View. *ca.* 540 B.C.

Drawn by Charles E. Brown

The Altar Court (Fig. 37) [14]

Situated to the south of the Hall of Votive Gifts and to the west of the southern half of the Hieron, it was an unroofed rectangular enclosure, *ca.* 14 meters from east to west by 17 meters from north to south. Its substructure is partly preserved on all sides. It was solidly built of limestone blocks of a variety also used in the foundation of the Propylon of Ptolemy II and was originally five courses high on all four sides. Over it the building rose to a height of *ca.* 8 meters.

The walls were built of stuccoed limestone on the eastern, southern, and northern sides. On the west, a marble Doric colonnade between marble antae formed a screen façade. The spacing of these columns with a wider interval in the center is approximately indicated by four drums which have been placed on the only preserved (lowest) foundation course of the façade. The walls were crowned by a marble course which carried the mouldings of the anta-capitals around the building. On this course and the columns rested a marble Doric entablature having a once-painted sima with lion's-head waterspouts. The intervals between the columns were closed by metal grilles and doors. The architrave bore the dedicatory inscription, probably of Arrhidaios, half-brother and eventual successor of Alexander the Great. Three large fragments of this inscription may be seen on the façade foundation.

The forepart of the enclosure was paved with a mosaic of diamond-shaped pieces of marble. Then steps ascended to a monumental marble altar, one cover slab of which may be seen in the interior. This altar was placed towards the rear, and its southern portion covered an Archaic sacrificial place on top of a huge outcropping of red and green porphyry rock. On top of this rock, part of a clay pipe that drained the liquid of sacrifices from the Archaic altar is still preserved. A

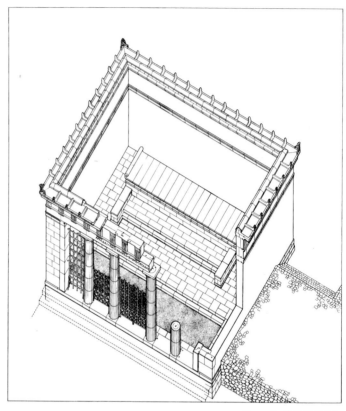

Fig. 37. The Altar Court. Restored View. *ca.* 340-330 B.C.

few meters in front of the façade several later walls are preserved. From about 200 B.C. on, they supported a wooden platform outside the building, the façade of which was then used, in spite of its different orientation, as a background for the theater performances.

In the Museum (Hall A), part of the entablature of the enclosure has been re-erected. A small section of the marble floor of the forepart of the court is exhibited in Case B3; an inscribed fragment of the Archaic pipeline in Case C11; fragments of stucco from the walls in Case C12.

An antefix and a fragmentary corner akroterion are preserved in the Ephesos-Museum in Vienna.

The Theater (Fig. 38) [13]

Built against the slope, the outline of its cavea is still recognizable, but its seats of white limestone and red porphyry were pillaged between 1927 and 1937. Two seats that escaped have been placed in the cavea. In antiquity, the riverbed was channeled through this area by rock retaining walls such as may be seen still partly upright farther south. During the summer festivals, a wooden orchestra floor must have covered this wide channel. In late antiquity, the ancient channel was converted into an underground concrete culvert and this culvert was restored after the excavation to protect the ruins from further destruction by the swollen spring torrent.

Above the ancient cavea the visitor saw the Nike of Samothrace (Fig. 5) and the southern end of the Stoa.

For the Theater, see Chapter II.

From the southeast corner of the Hieron, he may follow a path that leads eastwards, up the slope, to the Southern Nekropolis and then descends to cross the eastern torrent to the Propylon of Ptolemy II.

The Southern Nekropolis (Fig. 39) [27]

This is the most important of the cemeteries which have been explored thus far; other burial grounds have been partially excavated, including the area around and under the Hotel Xenia and the slopes outside the northwestern portion of the ancient city wall. In the limited space on this knoll,

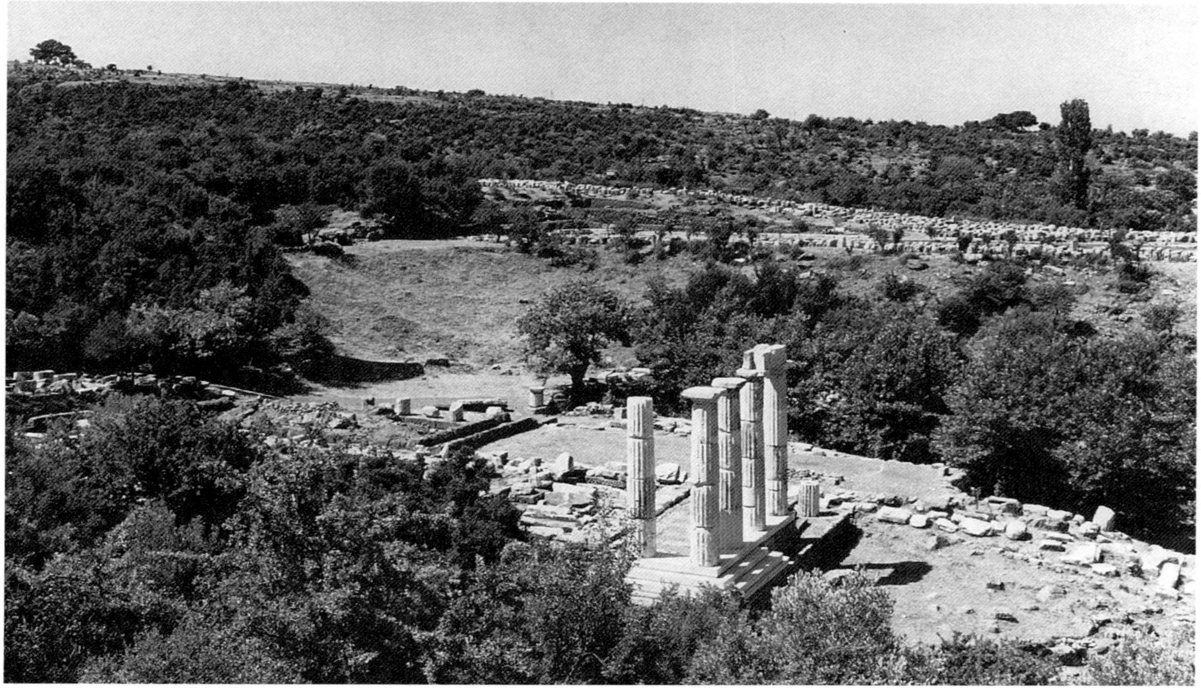

Photo Nicholas D. Ohly

Fig. 38. View of the Porch of the Hieron with the Theater Cavea, the Site of the Nike Monument and the Stoa in the Background.

Fig. 39. Inhumation Burial in the Southern Nekropolis.
First Century B.C.

more than four hundred tombs were found. They ranged in date from early in the Archaic period to the second century after Christ. The tombs of all periods were packed together in a thin layer below the modern ground level. The deepest parts of this stratum were only a little more than a meter thick and undisturbed earth lay everywhere below the burials. The tombs included cremation pots of various types as well as huge ceramic storage jars (pithoi), tombs built of stone slabs and shelters of large tiles, all used for inhumation burials (Fig. 39). Many of the vases and other objects from burials of all periods may be seen in the Museum (Halls C and D). Typical pithoi are stored in the courtyard.

Since the excavation, the cemetery has been partly refilled with earth and a rock retaining wall has been built on the stream side. All that remains visible on the site are the upper parts of some of the stone slab-tombs, a few fragments of rock walls, and a U-shaped foundation made of miscellaneous fragments from other structures which may have been part of a mausoleum. Near the road are various fragments of worked stone from small tomb monuments. One is a marble pediment with the bust of Psyche; another is a similar pediment with an eight-pointed star. The foundations of these little buildings have not been discovered.

Crossing the eastern ravine one reaches the Propylon of Ptolemy II.

The Propylon of Ptolemy II (Figs. 40, 54, 57) [26]

The limestone substructure which supported the Propylon built of Thasian marble is preserved except at its northwestern corner. This substructure is built on the steeply descending right bank of the river. It is a bold piece of Greek engineering distinguished by an oblique, barrel-vaulted tunnel that traverses the foundation in order to span the redirected bed of the seasonal torrent that, running from south to north, fixed the eastern boundary of the Sanctuary. At the western end of the foundation are the remains of two spur walls that, in Hellenistic times, supported a sloping causeway that linked the Propylon with the circular area on the Eastern Hill. As a result of the earthquake that destroyed the Hellenistic structures on that hill in the late first century or the second century after Christ, the course of the torrent sought again its original and present location, and, presumably, the Propylon was joined to the Sanctuary by a wooden bridge.

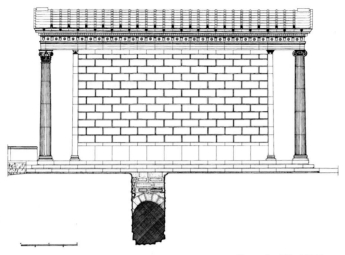

Drawn by Alfred K. Frazer

Fig. 40. Restored South Elevation of the Propylon of Ptolemy II.
285-281 B.C.

A road from the main gate of the city ended at a marble pavement in front of the Propylon, of which only the huge blocks of the border now remain. The marble building was 11.46 meters wide and 17.20 meters long at the stylobate. The amphiprostyle, pedimented gatehouse comprised two spacious porches facing east and west separated by a double door wall. These features, as well as the porous rails that once supported the marble pavements of the eastern and western porches, are readily seen today. The door wall was penetrated by a single portal less than two meters wide. The narrowness of the entrance, unusual in the gatehouses of Greek sanctuaries, may reflect a Samothracian rite that took place at the Sanctuary's entrance. The double thickness of the door wall created a chamber to the north and to the south of the portal. In the southern chamber, for reasons unknown, a simple stairway led to the attic. From the stylobate six Ionic columns rose above the three steps at the eastern end of the building facing the city; six Corinthian columns stood at the western end facing the Sanctuary. The latter represent the first documented appearance of the Corinthian column as an exterior, structural member in Greek architecture. On the architrave on both sides of the building, a large two-line inscription, "King Ptolemy, son of Ptolemy and Berenike the Saviors, to the Great Gods", announced this dedication by Ptolemy II Philadelphos (between 285 and 281 B.C.).

The marble blocks of the building's superstructure have been placed to the south and the north of the foundations. To the right of the path to the north lie four architrave blocks bearing most of the inscription from the eastern façade. Over the architrave, the building was adorned by a frieze carved with alternating bucranes and rosettes topped by dentils, a cornice, and a gutter with lion's-head waterspouts.

The building was partially excavated by the Austrians. Most of the decorative elements found at the time were taken to Vienna. Some frieze blocks are in the garden of the Archaeological Museum in Istanbul.

In the Museum in Samothrace, there are ornamental fragments, including one from a corner capital (Hall A). A plaster restoration of a typical Corinthian capital, based on numerous fragments of the original capitals, as well as one of the two original Corinthian anta capitals, is exhibited in Hall B. A fragment of the dedicatory inscription from the western façade is stored in the courtyard.

A fragmentary capital, fragments of the architrave and frieze, and an antefix are preserved in the Ephesos-Museum in Vienna.

Recrossing the ravine, the visitor may take a path on the right at the top of the ridge to visit the Eastern Hill of the Sanctuary.

The Eastern Hill (Figs. 41, 42) **[24-25]**

Immediately opposite the Propylon of Ptolemy II lies a complex of structures which must have served a now un-

Photo James R. McCredie
Fig. 41. View of the Eastern Hill from the South.

documented introductory rite at the entrance of the Sanctuary.

The center of the complex is occupied by a circular area (**25**), *ca.* 9 meters in diameter, flagged with irregular but well fitted fieldstone and limestone fragments. From it rose five encircling steps, of which the lower three or four are of fine hard limestone, while the top step is of friable coquina. These steps, too narrow for seats, must have provided places for spectators to stand, watching or participating in the proceedings centered on a marble altar in the middle of the pavement (now in Hall A of the Museum, see p. 122).

When the circular steps were constructed, sometime in the fifth century B.C., an opening *ca.* 2 meters wide led out from the paved area westward toward the central part of the Sanctuary. But at the end of the fifth century or early in the fourth century, the gap was filled, the steps reconstructed and made continuous, and the first of two successive rectan-

97

Fig. 42. Epistyle Blocks of the Dedication of Philip III and
Alexander IV.

gular buildings was added in the space thus made available
to the northwest. Fragments of its rubble walls are visible,
one at the south and one beneath the floor of its successor.
Though of ordinary construction, it was elaborately stuccoed
in red and white on the interior, with painted imitation of
drafted-margin masonry.

At the same time, a series of monument bases was begun,
of which foundations are visible at the south and west of the
reconstructed steps, probably to support bronze statues, of
which more than twenty bases were found nearby.

The stuccoed rubble building was replaced, between 323
and 317 B.C., by one far more elaborate —a marble, Doric,
hexastyle, prostyle structure (**24**). Its donors and date are
established by the dedicatory inscription, the beginning of
which is preserved on two epistyle blocks now at the south of
the round structure. It read: "Kings Philip (and) Alexander
to the Great Gods", recording the gift of Alexander the
Great's joint successors, his half-brother, Philip III Arrhidaios, and his posthumous, infant son, Alexander IV (Fig.
42).

Though badly pillaged, its foundations are clearly visible

on the site, and sufficient blocks of its superstructure remain to assure its reconstruction. The façade was carved in Pentelic(?) marble, and both in design and technique it shows a tradition apart from that of other Samothracian buildings. The side and back walls were, however, of the more usual Thasian marble, alternating on the interior with sandstone, where the walls must have been covered with stucco. The floor, partly preserved on the site, was of marble fragments set in a pattern in red cement. A tetrastyle Ionic porch, perhaps for the display of statues, was added somewhat later to the rear of the building.

After the construction of the Propylon of Ptolemy II between 285 and 281 B.C., a ramp led from that building to the circular, paved area; branching from it and leading north and westward, around it and the dedication of Philip and Alexander, a now vanished road connected with a paved, stepped way toward the Hall of Choral Dancers and the other buildings in the center of the Sanctuary.

Severe damage, apparently from an earthquake, caused a major revision of this new area in the late first or second century after Christ. The river found a new course between the Propylon of Ptolemy II and the Eastern Hill and necessitated the replacement of the earlier ramp with a wooden bridge, whose southwestern abutment, built of spoils from earlier monument foundations, is still preserved. The dedication of Philip and Alexander was thrown down over the circular pavement, and the road around the building was destroyed. No attempt was made to rebuild, and the debris was simply covered by earth to the level of the floor of the dedication of Philip and Alexander. The rites which this area had served may then have been omitted; if they continued, they were conducted henceforth, as perhaps in the earliest phase of the Sanctuary, without a monumental setting.

Following the ancient stepped ramp to regain the modern path above the Rotunda of Arsinoe the visitor has on

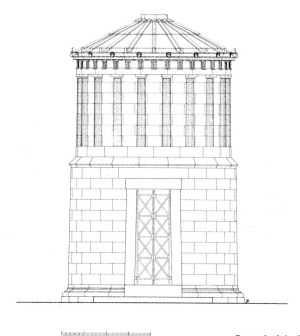

Drawn by John Kurtich
Fig. 43. Doric Rotunda. Restored Elevation. 350-300 B.C.

his right, at the highest point of the path, a hollow which marks the remnants of the foundation, now reburied to protect it, of a tiny but remarkable round Doric building.

Doric Rotunda (Figs. 43-45) **[28]**

Though poorly preserved, owing both to ancient destruction and pillage and to the extremely friable character of the material, enough survived to determine the general features of the structure and to permit a tentative restoration. Its foundation is a circle, *ca.* 4.10 meters in diameter, from which a rectangle, *ca.* 2.70 meters wide, extends toward the northwest, apparently for a ramp. Large flattened fieldstones

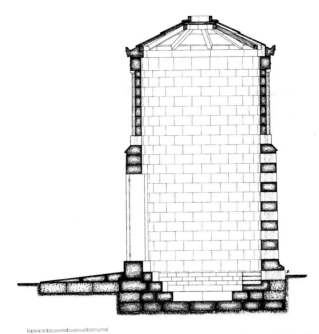

Drawn by John Kurtich

Fig. 44. Doric Rotunda. Restored Cross-section. 350-300 B.C.

form the base of the circle and, within, the floor of the structure. The superstructure, including the roof, was entirely of
gray-brown marine limestone, of which only few and small,
but telling, fragments survive.

From a boldly molded toichobate rose the drum of the
lower wall, pierced by a doorway. This drum was capped by
a simply molded course, upon which stood the upper drum,
decorated with an engaged Doric order of eighteen columns,
of which the component parts are all represented, if scantily,
among the preserved fragments. Within, three steps led down
to the solid floor; in a later remodelling the two upper steps
were replaced by a single shelf composed of three courses of
wedge-shaped bricks or tiles.

Photo James R. McCredie
Fig. 45. Doric Rotunda. 350-300 B.C.

Both architectural details and material from its foundation ditch suggest that this building was constructed in the second half, perhaps the fourth quarter of the fourth century. Although the type recalls monumental tombs of Classical and Hellenistic Asia Minor, as well as the nearby but later Rotunda of Arsinoe, its solid floor and limited space make it unsuitable for sacrifice to chthonic deities and for burial. If the funereal associations are real, it might have served as a cenotaph, but there is no hint as to whose.

Proceeding southward along the path, which crosses the central torrent of the Sanctuary and climbs westward, behind the Hieron, the visitor will reach the upper terrace of the Western Hill, at the top of the Theater.

The Nike Monument (Figs. 5, 46) [12]

At the south of the terrace stands a fragment of boulder retaining wall, oblique to the neighboring Stoa and apparently earlier. Set into it is the open horseshoe of terrace

Fig. 46. View of the Ruins of the Nike Monument.

walls added in Early Imperial times to protect the monument dominated by the Victory of Samothrace (Fig. 46). The latter is a rectangle of limestone facing north and subdivided in the center by a cross wall. At the back one sees traces (running obliquely from the rear wall toward the northeast) of the foundation on which marble slabs with rippled surface supported the gray marble ship's prow bearing the figure of Victory in Parian marble dating from the early second century B.C. (Fig. 5). Seen against the sky, she seemed to have alighted on the ship.

In 1863 Champoiseau found the statue lying broken in pieces as it had fallen forward from its high position. The right hand was discovered in 1950.

Just west of the Nike Monument stand the remains of the Stoa.

Photo James R. McCredie
Fig. 47. View of the Stoa from the South.

The Stoa (Figs. 47, 48) [**11**]

This long portico, the largest building in the Sanctuary, loomed conspicuously above the complex of older cult buildings and gave architectural definition to the western side of the Sanctuary. Its imposing size led early investigators to interpret the ruins as the "Great Temple" of Samothrace, but more extensive tests by the Austrian expedition revealed its true character as a stoa built in the first half of the third century B.C. to shelter the increasingly numerous visitors to the Sanctuary. The entire building has now been laid bare, and the nearly 1500 fallen blocks of its superstructure found in the excavations stand to the east, south, and west of the foundations.

The building extends *ca.* 104 meters from north to south and *ca.* 13.40 meters from east to west. The size of the Stoa required its builders artificially to enlarge the hill on which it stands, and at the north the natural level was raised by more than five meters. The building occupies nearly the whole length of the area thus created for it; at the south, a narrow passage separates it from the massive terrace wall built of boulders which supported higher ground on the south and west; at the north, the hill extended only about four meters beyond the building, where the preserved eastern part of a

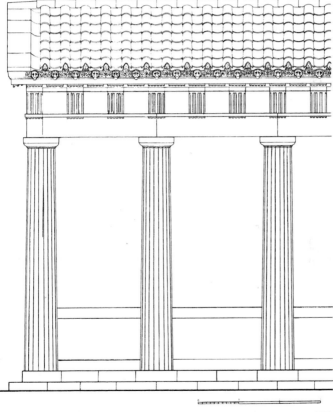

Drawn by Nicholas D. Ohly

Fig. 48. Reconstruction of a Section of the Façade of the Stoa.
300-250 B.C.

105

strong terrace wall which formed the northern boundary of the area still stands. A number of monuments stood on the broad terrace to the east of the façade; for the most part, only their foundations are *in situ*, but the southernmost also retains its lowest marble course. To one of these foundations belongs the monument of Philip V, dedicated by the Macedonians to the Great Gods about 200 B.C., of which the base and the capital of its supporting Doric column are stored in the courtyard of the Museum.

The limestone foundations of the Stoa are well preserved except at the northern end, where as many as six courses have been pillaged. At the south, where virgin soil lay near the surface, only a shallow foundation was needed; but at the north, the foundations had to descend five meters or more to reach virgin soil, and here the limestone courses are laid on a subfoundation of boulders. A similar scheme was used for the foundations of the interior colonnade; remains of the boulder subfoundations for the seven northernmost columns are preserved, though the cut limestone foundations themselves have been pillaged. A small portion of the euthynteria and toichobate courses remains *in situ* near the southwest corner, where a heavy covering of fallen blocks protected it from stone robbers.

The façade had a single step, upon which stood a colonnade of 35 Doric columns surmounted by a Doric entablature; the rinceau gutter with lion's-head waterspouts, the palmette antefixes, and the roof tiles were all of terracotta. The north, south, and west sides of the building were formed by walls which terminated in antae behind the corner columns of the façade and in engaged pilasters at the rear corners; it is probable that doorways in the rear western wall gave access to the broad open area behind the Stoa. The limestone masonry was covered with fine white marble stucco, thus giving the building the appearance of marble.

Within the Stoa a row of 16 Ionic columns, terminating in

an engaged Ionic half-column at each end, supported a wooden architrave upon which rested the roof timbers. The floor was of earth and the walls were stuccoed and painted red, white, and blue-grey or black to imitate masonry; inscriptions, seemingly recording lists of initiates, were incised on the stucco.

Only a few rubble walls buried by the Stoa fill attest to earlier activity on the Western Hill. No evidence of a monumental predecessor of the Stoa was found. Later additions were also of a less monumental character; the rubble walls of a small, two-roomed structure built against the rear wall of the Stoa in the fourth century after Christ and remains of a frequently repaired water system may be seen at the southwest of the building.

In the Museum (Case B3), a restored piece of the terracotta sima and two complete antefixes are exhibited. Pottery from debris incorporated in the fill of the terrace in front of the Stoa is on view (Cases C7 and C8), and the capital and statue base of the monument of Philip V is installed in the courtyard. At the time of the Austrian excavations, the ruin of a medieval tower built over the Stoa of spoils from the ancient structure was dismantled.

Several fragments of the terracotta sima, lion's-head waterspouts, and an antefix are preserved in the Ephesos-Museum in Vienna.

The visitor may cross the foundations of the Stoa and descend by a path at its northwest corner to the middle terrace of the Western Hill.

The Western Hill (Figs. 49-52) [**1-13**]

Recent excavations have shown that this terrace and the sloping ground to its west were occupied by three substantial ancient buildings, partly obscured by the remains of a Byzantine establishment.

At the eastern edge of the terrace stood a monumental

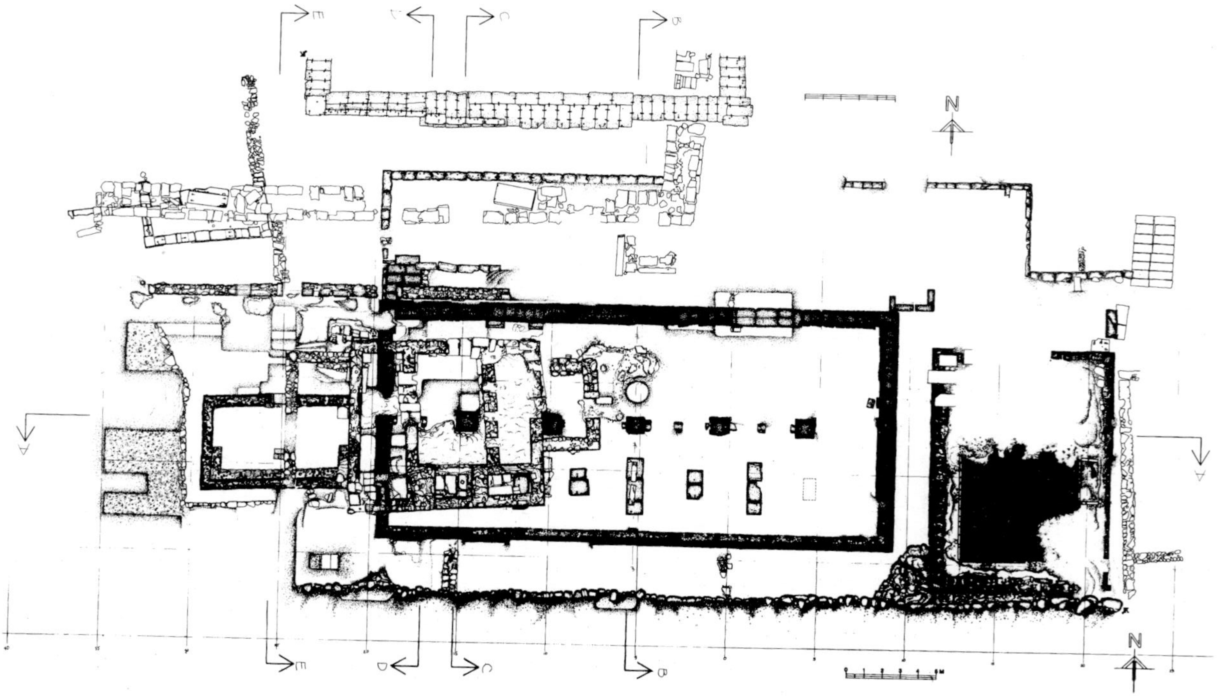

Fig. 49. Actual-state Plan of the Neorion and Environs.

Drawn by John Kurtich

108

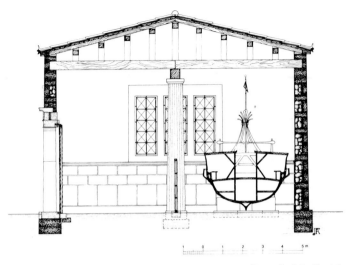

Drawn by John Kurtich

Fig. 50. Restored Cross-section of the Neorion. *ca.* 250 B.C.

dining room or *hestiatorion* which, like the Milesian dedication and other rooms on this hill (see below), accommodated the ritual meal that accompanied the rites of initiation. Although the walls of this structure were robbed out in late antiquity, its floor is preserved (now covered with earth to protect it), a fine but patternless mosaic of marble chips. Along the walls stood a slightly raised platform, edged with reused marble cover-tiles, to accommodate the dining couches; at the west similar tiles, inverted, formed drains to aid in cleaning the floor. The room was probably square, with eleven couches, and preceded by an anteroom, but the now incomplete foundations do not rule out a single rectangular room. Originally constructed toward the middle of the third century B.C., the present floor belongs to a later revision, perhaps in the Early Imperial period.

Next to the *hestiatorion*, occupying the remainder of the

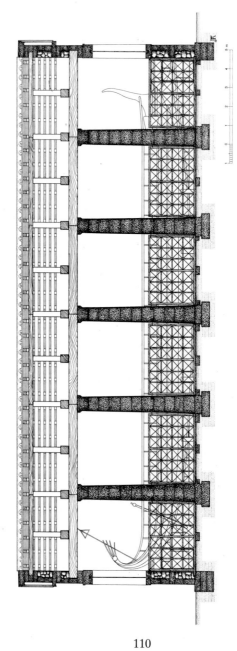

Fig. 51. Restored Longitudinal Section of the Neorion. *ca.* 250 B.C.

Drawn by John Kurtich

terrace, stood a *neorion*, a large rectangular building to house the dedication of a ship, probably a warship. Enclosed by walls on all sides, it was entered through two marble doorways in its northern long side, and triple windows in the front and side walls provided additional illumination. The interior was divided longitudinally into two aisles by a row of five columns joined by a screen or grille. The inner, southern aisle was provided with a series of seven foundations for marble supports which cradled the ship; the central pair stands nearly in place, and others were reused in medieval buildings. Though the building was hastily constructed in order to shelter the ship as quickly as possible, the monument must have been one of the most imposing in the Sanctuary. The dedicant remains unknown, but the Macedonian style of architecture and its date in the second quarter of the third century B.C. suggests Antigonos Gonatas, who developed Macedonian sea power.

To the west of the *neorion* stood a smaller rectangular building of Roman Imperial date. Two marble bases in its floor and a bench or shelf along its back and side walls probably supported statuary or other dedications.

From the crossroads, north of the stairway, a broad ancient path led westward across the lower northern terrace of the Western Hill.

At the east of this terrace lie the foundations of a large marble building (**6**); its square central room was entered through an Ionic porch at the south and was flanked on each side by a slightly smaller square room. Enough of the dedicatory inscription was preserved from the epistyle of the porch to identify the donor as a woman from Miletos, but her name is still unknown, as is the name of the building. Only the similarity of its plan to dining complexes at such sites as Pella and Vergina suggests that it, too, was constructed for that purpose, apparently in the second half of the third century B.C.

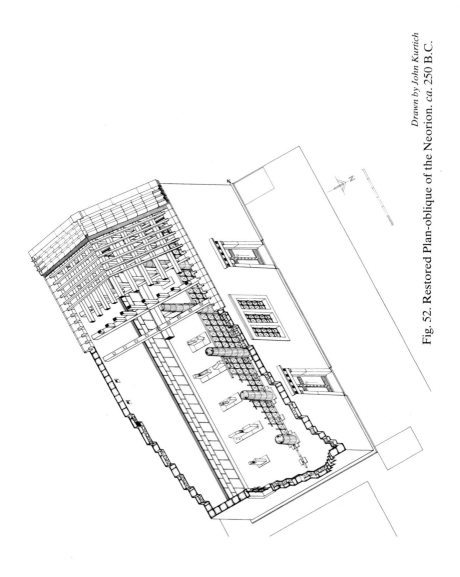

Fig. 52. Restored Plan-oblique of the Neorion. *ca.* 250 B.C.

Various elements of superstructure are collected south of the building, while others remain among the spoils reused in Byzantine walls to the west. Part of the dedicatory inscription preserved in the nineteenth century is now lost; two surviving fragments are in the courtyard of the Museum.

Immediately west of the Milesian dedication are the foundations of an even larger building, now partly obscured by Byzantine walls (**4**). Though it was never completed and apparently stood as an open platform to the end of antiquity, its intended form can be recovered from the foundations, with the help of marble blocks reused in medieval walls. The marble euthynteria is still in place at the south; above it rose a crepidoma of three marble steps, widened at the north and south ends to support colonnaded entrances. An unfinished anta base shows that the order was to be Ionic. The entrances were to lead to a shallow antechamber at each end, which, in turn, led to the large central room, *ca.* 19 meters long and 21.50 meters wide. Foundations had been laid for two rows of interior columns to support the roof. To judge from its workmanship, the structure was begun in the late fourth century or early third century B.C. and soon abandoned.

Further to the west, between this unfinished building and the western stream bed, three simple buildings of local sandstone were added in later Hellenistic times (**1-3**). Each comprised a rectangular room entered by a porch, either prostyle or *in antis*. The northernmost and southernmost buildings faced south, while the central building faced north. In plan and arrangement they resemble the treasuries at Delphi or Olympia, but their identification is still uncertain. Fragmentary walls attest to the presence of additional structures south of these buildings in Roman times, though none of monumental character.

In the tenth century after Christ, long after the abandoned Sanctuary had fallen into ruins, this area was reoccupied for military purposes, and a fort was constructed over both the platform of the unfinished building and its three smaller neighbors to the west, mainly of spoils from these and nearby structures (**5**). It formed a rough square, *ca.* 36 by 39 meters, with towers projecting from each corner toward the north and south; the now demolished entrance stood on the east. A number of rooms or houses in the western half of the enclosure presumably sheltered its garrison. The events which led to the construction of this fort apparently soon passed, and within a century buildings spread outside the walls. They, too, were abandoned before long, and the site saw only desultory later occupation.

The modern path northward from the Theater leads past an adjoining area at the base of the western ridge, below the Stoa, and toward the lower, northern terrace of the Western Hill. The path approximates the line of a broad road along the central stream of the Sanctuary which connected these areas in antiquity. Remains are visible of the massive concrete retaining wall which, in Roman times, supported this road while controlling the course of the river, and a few boulders just behind it mark the position of its early Hellenistic predecessor.

The eastern slope of the Stoa's ridge and the strip between it and the central stream were repeatedly built upon and revised in contour from the late fourth century B.C., when this area was added to the Sanctuary, to the end of antiquity.

The first major construction in this area was a building for ritual dining (**7**). *Ca.* 22 meters long, set against and partly into the northern end of the slope, from which its back wall was separated by a narrow drainage space, it faced the older cult buildings across the stream. It comprised three rooms, each *ca.* 6.50 meters square, which probably opened onto a now vanished porch at the east. In the two lateral rooms, a marble border framed a central pavement of marble chips and set it off from the meter-wide strip along the walls, upon which dining couches will have stood; a paving of pebbles set in cement covered the entire floor of the central room. Only the lowest parts of the preserved walls, built of cut and well-fitted fieldstones, belong to the original fourth-century form of this building. The prominent concrete superstructure stems from repairs and rebuilding in the first and second centuries A.D. and later, when the slope behind the building was also filled and levelled.

A small square room was added at the north of the building in the late Hellenistic period, and north of it a large room, 9.60 meters square, was added in the second century after Christ, perhaps to replace a Classical or Hellenistic structure; both rooms, to judge from their shape, may also have served for dining.

Southward of these buildings, between them and the Theater, there seems always to have been an indentation in the hillside, but in the late third or early second century B.C., the area was expanded and regularized by the construction of a strong retaining wall, some 7 meters high and 24 meters long, set back into the slope. Built of panels of polygonal fieldstones alternating with string-courses of cut sandstone blocks and strengthened by four sandstone buttresses, it formed one of the most impressive examples of masonry in the Sanctuary. At the south, this retaining wall turns eastward to support the slope which again rises toward the Theater's cavea, where two additional square rooms of yet uncertain purpose were constructed (**8, 10**). Built into this return where it joins the main wall is a curious niche (**9**). With a huge fieldstone lintel and, over it, a relieving triangle framed by sandstone blocks, it reproduces the appearance of a Mycenaean door, such as regularly occurs in tholos tombs. Within the entrance, the jambs continue some 1.50 meters to meet a wall built against bedrock. The impression of venerable age which the construction of this niche gives it is surely intentional, and it may have been connected in Hellenistic times with a Samothracian legend of the heroic age. Other remains in this area belong to several later phases of building.

North of the structures just described, the modern path continues through a depression caused by erosion after the retaining walls along the river had collapsed. Turning westward, the visitor again climbs to the ancient level at a crossroads. A stairway, flanked by the foundations of monuments, led upwards to a terrace intermediate between this level and that of the Stoa.

IV

The Museum

The Building

The building of a local museum was begun by the American expedition immediately after full excavation in the heart of the Sanctuary had been determined upon and with the understanding that the Greek government would ultimately receive ownership of and administer this museum. Funds for its construction and installation were donated to New York University primarily by one generous American donor. The designs were made by Stuart M. Shaw of the Metropolitan Museum of Art in New York.

Construction of the major hall was begun in 1939 with the aid of a contribution from an anonymous sponsor. During the war, the building material was looted and objects temporarily kept in a nearby storage room were damaged, some being destroyed, others stolen, and much valuable information was obliterated.

The major hall was completed in 1948. The southern and western wings of the building were added and the Museum installed in 1953 and 1954. In style and arrangement, the Museum is adapted to the protection and exhibition of local antiquities. Though most of the material was unearthed in the American excavations, it also contains many items accidentally found by local residents since 1939 and a number of antiquities previously assembled in the main church of Chora by the late Dr. Phardys, as well as others dispersed in various parts of the island in post-antique times. Following an agreement between the Greek and the French governments, three valuable items belonging to the Louvre are exhibited on permanent loan and, in return, the right hand of the Victory of Samothrace has been loaned to the Louvre.

As it is installed, this Museum is not primarily a treasure house of valuable *objets d'art*, though it does contain many fine pieces of the minor and decorative arts as well as a few masterpieces of Greek sculpture. It aims, above all, at illustrating major features of local civilization and at supplementing the picture gained in the excavation by an exhibition of objects that throw light on the history of the Sanctuary and its religion.

The building itself is constructed in a style adapted to the local scene. The Museum was opened in July of 1955. The northern wing was built in 1960-61, thanks to the generous sponsorship of an American philanthropic foundation.

In the central hall (A), architectural features of the major buildings of the Sanctuary have been reconstructed. Halls B and C, to the south, are mainly dedicated to sculptures and minor objects. Finds from the nekropolis, ultimately to be installed in Hall E, are provisionally exhibited in Halls C and D. The western wing contains offices. Inscriptions are stored in the courtyard framed by the four wings, and other materials are in storerooms. These materials, not on exhibition, are available to specialists with the permission of the excavators or the Museum authorities.

Hall A

The architectural restorations in this hall aim to give a visual experience of outstanding features of some of the major buildings. The individual blocks used in these reconstructions were not necessarily placed next to or on top of each other in antiquity as they appear here. In each instance, the reconstruction presents a typical section of the building.

To the right of the main door (a): fragments of the superstructure of the Hall of Votive Gifts. Gray imported limestone. A few finely worked wall blocks carefully prepared for the stucco coating that still adheres to them in patches.

Above, cornice blocks and, in the center, one resting on pedimental stones. *ca.* 540 B.C.

For the building, see above, pp. 86ff.

To the left of the main door (b): partial reconstruction of the entablature of the Altar Court, probably dedicated by Arrhidaios. The Doric entablature of the exterior rests on a molded upper course crowning the enclosure walls which is repeated on the interior, with less projection (see rear of reconstruction). The gutter, lacking plastic decoration, was painted in antiquity. In the center, traces of a lion's-head waterspout. Of the two antefixes, the left one is original, the right one a plaster cast. Between 340 and 330 B.C.

For the structure, see above, pp. 89ff.

On the opposite wall (c): partial reconstruction of the entablature of the Hieron. Above, the gutter with rinceau decoration, a lion's-head waterspout, and two marble antefixes: the left one from the Hellenistic period, the right one dating from a Roman reconstruction. *ca.* 325 B.C.

Next to the entablature, against the south wall (e): part of the base of the central akroterion which crowned the rear pediment. Below, windswept acanthus leaves; thick stalks with lateral shoots curled upward, their virtuoso openwork seen against the blue sky, supporting palmettes and flowers, fragments of which are exhibited in Case 1, to the left of the entrance to Hall B. On the wall over this case (f), a fragment of the raking sima of the rear pediment. Above the door to Hall B (g), a plaster reconstruction of the Hellenistic central akroterion which crowned each pediment (drawing showing extant fragments on the wall below, Fig. 53). 150-125 B.C.

For the building, see above, pp. 79ff.

On the wall to the right of the Hieron entablature (d): the upper part of a marble stele which prohibited entry by the uninitiated into the Hieron.

In the center of the western wall, opposite the main door (h): a section of the entablature of the Rotunda of Arsinoe.

Fig. 53. Reconstruction of the Hellenistic Central Akroterion of
the Hieron. 150-125 B.C.

On the outer convex face the entablature is Doric, crowned
by a fragmentary gutter with rinceaux and a lion's-head
waterspout. Over its joint, an antefix. On the wall to the left

of the entablature (i), a fragment of the gutter with its lion's-head waterspout.

The entablature was scaled to the height of the whole Rotunda rather than to that of the decorative gallery which it crowned. A section of the gallery has been re-erected in the center of the northern part of the hall (j). Supported by ancient wall blocks crowned by a fine double-faced anthemion frieze and a Lesbian cymation, it exhibits three pilasters. On the exterior they are unfluted and have anta-like capitals, but on the interior they have the form of Corinthian half-columns. The lower intervals are occupied by parapets decorated with bucranes and rosettes; those of the interior, by altars adorned with bucranes and paterae (Fig. 13). Above, the intercolumniations were closed by thin screens. On top of the gallery, the lower part of the architrave is indicated in plaster and cement. Between 288 and 281 B.C.

In the corner behind the gallery and to the right (k), fragments of the marble finial decorated with laurel leaves from the Roman roof (the upper fragment on permanent loan from the Louvre) and, on the wall, a scale-shaped tile from the Hellenistic roof of the Rotunda.

For the building, see above, pp. 62ff.

Behind the gallery and to its left (n) is a reconstruction of a section of the edge of the roof of the Anaktoron with flat eaves-tiles and cover tiles incorporating palmette antefixes. Early Imperial.

See above, pp. 31, 42, 56ff.

On the wall to its left (o), a fragmentary Ionic corner capital from the Propylon of Ptolemy II (see above, p. 94 ff.) and, further to the left (l), a beautifully carved Early Hellenistic S-shaped bracket which once supported the lintel of a door.

Below them (m), the marble stele (Fig. 11) which stood between the two doors leading from the main hall to the rear sanctuary of the Anaktoron and, in Latin and Greek, forbade entry of the uninitiated: *Deorum sacra qui non acceperunt non intrant.* Ἀμύητον μὴ εἰσιέναι. At the lower right, the kerykeion, symbol of Hermes Kadmilos, between two snakes alluding to the twin Kabeiroi-Dioskouroi. The lower part of the stele is rough and was inserted into the steps leading up to the doors. Early Imperial.

In the center of the hall (p), a finely ornamented circular marble altar found on the Eastern Hill where it may have stood at the center of the paved ritual area in the fourth or third century B.C. (see p. 96ff).

Hall B

In the center (h): a plaster reconstruction of a Corinthian capital and base from the western porch of the Propylon of Ptolemy II (Fig. 54; see above, pp. 94ff.). 285-281 B.C.

To the right of the entrance from Hall A (a): a monolithic Ionic column of Thasian marble from the Hall of Choral Dancers has been erected. The base, of unknown form, is missing. Over the shaft, a singular drum with a pattern com-

Photo James R. McCredie
Fig. 54. Reconstruction of a Corinthian Capital from the Propylon of Ptolemy II. 285-281 B.C.

Photo Anna Wachsmann.
Fig. 55. Capital and Drum from the Hall of Choral Dancers. *ca.* 340 B.C.

posed of flame palmettes, alternately upright and pendant, linked by extensions of their own tendrils form bold, curvilinear frames. These tightly juxtaposed elements once sprang from a ring of acanthus leaves at the base of the drum and it was also bordered at the top by an orthodox bead-and-reel molding. Above it, a fragmentary capital decorated with an anthemion bolster pattern framed by bead-and-reel borders (Fig. 55). Opposite this column, near the south wall (b), fragments of another such capital are exhibited on top of a second fragmentary necking block. Along the walls flanking the entrance to Hall C (c), blocks of the sculptured marble frieze of this building are exhibited. This frieze represents choruses of dancers clasping each other at the wrists. They move in two directions, and once encircled the building, converging on a lost central portion of the frieze. The best preserved block, at the left, with twelve complete figures, shows a female cithara player among the dancers (Fig. 33). It was found in 1949 where it had fallen, outside the Hall of Choral Dancers, as was the fragmentary block at the right. The two slabs immediately to the right of the door are the front parts of complete blocks which were sawed off at the back in modern times. These slabs, plundered from the

123

Sanctuary, were reused decoratively in the Gattilusi towers in the fifteenth century (Frontispiece), when they were seen and drawn by Cyriacus of Ancona (photograph to right of door to Hall C) and interpreted by him as representing the nine Muses and "The Samothracian Nymphs". They include a tympanum player and a flutist. The slabs are badly worn from their long exposure until 1863, at which time they were taken to the Louvre, whence they have been returned to Samothrace as a permanent loan.

The missing central scene probably referred to the wedding of Kadmos and Harmonia. Each girl in the frieze wears on her head a low polos, the headgear reserved for divinity, especially the Great Goddess in her many forms and her mortal votaries, and a kind of mantle worn only for ceremonial actions. In allusion to the remote antiquity of the event, the artist has represented these figures in archaistic style, thus blending the decorative forms of Archaic drapery with the swift and graceful elegance of his own period. The frieze is the earliest example of the extensive use of the archaistic style in Greek sculpture. *ca.* 340 B.C.

For the Hall of Choral Dancers, see above, pp. 73ff.

To the left of the entrance from Hall A (d and e): two sculptures of Thasian marble found in the central riverbed of the Sanctuary, probably part of a pedimental group from an unknown building, possibly the building antedating the Hellenistic Hieron. The bust (Fig. 56) originally represented the blind seer Teiresias who, stooping forward, emerges from the underworld (the eyes were recut in the nineteenth century, when the bust was used as an icon of a protective saint in the façade of a house in Chora). Around his head, the fillet of a priest. The bust was seen and drawn in a much better preserved state in 1444 by Cyriacus of Ancona (photograph on the wall next to it), who interpreted it as a portrait of Aristotle both because of its eyes, which he took to be unusually small rather than closed to indicate blindness,

Photo Anna Wachsmann.
Fig. 56. Marble Bust of Teiresias.
ca. 460 B.C.

and because of the hair of the skull bound by a fillet which he thought was a skullcap, and as such, it became a model for Renaissance portraits of the great philosopher.

The full-length figure, probably from the center of the pediment and representing Persephone, is clad in a peplos. The head is missing. The scene evidently represented the *Nekyia*, the descent of Odysseus into the underworld, as narrated by Homer and painted at the time of these sculptures by Polygnotos of Thasos.

Both figures are badly worn from more than a millennium of erosion in the riverbed, but they still exhibit the character of early Classical sculpture of the Island School and were probably made by a Thasian sculptor. *ca.* 460-450 B.C.

Case 1 contains various elements throwing light on the religion of the Sanctuary and its rites, typical votive gifts, and some pieces illustrating Greek technical procedures.

Top shelf, left section: in the background, top of a marble image of Hekate Zerynthia, found in the Sanctuary (see above, p. 30). In front, left to right, a hemispherical marble symbol, one of a number found near the Hieron (ompha-

125

los?); an iron ring with a carnelian engraved with a cock and a bunch of grapes; two molded fragments and a roughly shaped amulet of a black, resinous material (the Samothracian "Black Stone", see above, p. 16); a Samothracian iron finger ring found in the Sanctuary (see above, pp. 30, 38; another such ring found in a tomb of the Southern Nekropolis is exhibited in Hall D, Case 5); a piece of hematite containing natural iron ore from a smelting process, from the Sanctuary.

Center: in the background, a small, round inscribed altar dedicated to the Great Gods by ambassadors (ΘΕΩΡΟΙ) from Paros (see above, p. 34), found near the Rotunda of Arsinoe and dating from the second century B.C.; a ring-stone of blue glass with the representation of a goddess of half-iconic Anatolian type with a tall, narrow polos on her head (Axiokersa-Persephone?, see above, p. 33); photograph of the bezel of a silver ring found in the Sanctuary and stolen during World War II, incised with two snakes and two stars, symbols of the Kabeiroi-Dioskouroi (see above, p. 31ff); a Samothracian bronze coin with Axieros-Demeter enthroned and attended by a lion (Fig. 8).

Right side: two Hellenistic terracotta heads showing young women wearing tall, narrow poloi (Axiokersa-Persephone?, see above, p. 33); head of a veiled woman, probably an initiate (Fig. 19 and p. 41 above); two Hellenistic heads, the one on the right (Fig. 12) found in the Sanctuary, the left one in a tomb, showing a bearded divinity, probably Axiokersos-Hades (see above, p. 33); a finger-shaped clay object (symbol?) found in the Sanctuary; at the right, part of a crescent-shaped clay symbol (of Hekate-Zerynthia?) and part of a horn-shaped clay symbol, both found in the Sanctuary.

Second shelf, votive gifts. At the left: votive gifts found in the Sanctuary: two bronze fishhooks; a bronze arrow-head; a sea-shell perforated for suspension; a fragment of an alabaster oil flask (alabastron); two fragments of bone boxes;

two sets of knucklebones (astragals) from a wild and a tame goat found in the Sanctuary.

Center: a typical group of vessels used in the rites: a kantharos; a skyphos; two bowls, one stamped ΘΕ, an abbreviation for Θεῶν, "(property) of the Gods"; a saltcellar inscribed with the shorter form Θ (see below, p. 151); and fragmentary terracottas which were dedications in the Sanctuary, including the lower part of a freely modeled statuette of a man, *ca.* 350 B.C., head with mask of a comic actor, horse's head, and two Rhodian figurines, a reclining banqueter and a grotesque, of the 6th century B.C.

At the right: a bowl and a number of fragments of marble bowls (paterae) and basins dedicated in the Sanctuary.

Third shelf, at the left: an ivory spoon, an ivory handle, a fragment of a cylindrical ivory box, and a bronze needle; a circular clay vase of the Archaic period, deformed during its manufacture, but actually used; a fragment of a big clay vessel broken and repaired in antiquity with lead clamps.

Center: a bronze chisel and nail; bronze and iron clamps, three of them in the lead pourings by which they were fastened into marble building blocks; two bronze dowels for the vertical connecting of building blocks, one of them within part of the lead pouring which kept it in position; three lead objects which may have been archetypes for molds used in casting bronze objects (a bronze door stud is shown next to one of lead); a bronze door pan for the lower pin of the main door of the Anaktoron (see above, p. 59).

At the right: a lead pan for the lower pin of a door set into a stone socket, from the Hall of Votive Gifts; an inscribed and stamped lead weight; a selection of terracotta weights; a lead fishing net weight; kiln supports, of which numerous examples were found in the Sanctuary.

Bottom shelf, at the left: lower part of a circular terracotta altar found *in situ* to the south of the Rotunda of Arsinoe and dating from the sixth century B.C.; in the center, a fragment from the upper end of a large marble candelabrum imitating a huge torch with the head of a snake whose body was entwined about the shaft, from the interior installation of the Hieron. At the right, a fragment of the base slab of a circular marble altar or column with a finely carved guilloche pattern, dating from the late fifth or the fourth century B.C.

Case 2 contains a selection of coins and roof tile fragments marked by a stamp or incised letter.

At the left, Samothracian coins: above, eight silver coins of the sixth century B.C. (with the head of the city patroness Athena, a sphinx, a lion's head). The bronze coins date from the Hellenistic and Roman periods. They show the head of Athena on the obverse and, on the reverse, the seated goddess with one of her attendant lions, a ram's head and kerykeion, or a ship's prow (see above, pp. 22, 31ff.).

In the center, coins of Ainos, Athens, Histiaia, and Maroneia, a coin with the head of Alexander the Great as Herakles, and Roman Imperial coins, including a silver coin of Trajan. Below, a medal of King Otto commemorating the liberation of Greece.

At the right, fragments of stamped and inscribed roof tiles: Ἱερὰ Θεῶν (sacred to the Gods) from an ancient storeroom for roof tiles close to the Sanctuary. Another fragment (probably ἱερὰ Θεῶν) from the roof of the Sacristy; others, "Of the Gods" (Θεῶν). Below, stamped tiles from the Rotunda of Arsinoe and the Hieron.

Case 3 contains chiefly architectural fragments.

Top shelf: terracotta sima with rinceaux and a lion's-head waterspout (lower part, with tongue, restored) and two terracotta antefixes from the Stoa (see above, p. 106). First half of the third century B.C.

Second shelf, left section and front center: two fragmentary Archaic antefixes from unknown structures in the Sanctuary or the town, and two antefixes found in the Anaktoron from the fifth century B.C.

Center: three fragmentary terracotta antefixes, probably from the predecessor of the Hieron (*ca.* 460-450 B.C.).

Right section: terracotta antefix, without relief decoration, from the ridge of a roof and two fragments of terracotta antefixes from the ridge of the Hieron (see above, p. 82).

Third shelf, left section: a light limestone piece decorated with a star and a section of the marble mosaic floor from the forepart of the Altar Court, 340-330 B.C. (see above, p. 89). To the rear, one of a number of Greek bricks found in the Sanctuary and antedating the third century B.C.

Center: fragmentary inscribed sundial which marked both the hour of the day and the season of the year. Hellenistic.

Right section: fragment of a marble candelabrum(?) from the Hall of Choral Dancers, *ca.* 340 B.C. (a larger fragment of the same monument is in Vienna); a piece of a finely carved Lesbian cymation from an altar or base, fourth century B.C.; a fragment of a marble gutter with rinceau decoration in perspective, from the Hall of Choral Dancers (see above, p. 75; other fragments in Vienna); fragmentary marble antefix from an unknown building in the Sanctuary, Hellenistic period.

Bottom shelf, at left: fragment of a large marble door bracket with rinceau decoration at the side. Hellenistic.

Center: a fragmentary lion's-head waterspout from the Hall of Choral Dancers, *ca.* 340 B.C. (for the Propylon, see above, pp. 73ff); fragmentary marble block with sloping upper edge from a structure (altar?) with relief decoration, possibly part of the representation of a Doric building. Found in the Anaktoron.

Right section: fragments of terracotta sarcophagi of the

Archaic and Classical periods, possibly destroyed during an expansion of the Sanctuary.

To the right of Case 3, on the wall (f): fragments of two Greek stelai, the first and more fragmentary one drawn by Cyriacus of Ancona in 1444, who saw it when it was complete (Fig. 7; photograph here at left), the other representing in greater detail the image of a round building, its door flanked by snake-entwined torches, its frieze decorated by bucranes and garlands, which bears inscriptions on its sides presumably to supplement a missing text on its front. Both stelai were probably dedicated in the Sanctuary by residents of Kyzikos and show a building related to the early Hellenistic Rotunda of Arsinoe, possibly a later local branch Samothrakion for initiates residing in Kyzikos (see above, p. 69). Only citizens of that city seem to have used this image on the inscriptions recording their initiation.

The more fragmentary stele includes the names of individuals delegated to offer sacrifices in Samothrace on behalf of their town (see above, p. 34) and all were *mystai*. Names of initiates in the higher degree, *epoptai*, are inscribed on each side of the building in ovals which probably represent the purple scarf worn by Samothracian initiates (see above, p. 38). Below these ovals, to the left and right of the building, a Roman, Quintus Visellius, recorded his visit at a later time, calling himself one "pious in prayer". The fragments of this inscription may be restored with the help of copies of Cyriacus' drawing.

Both inscriptions date from the late Hellenistic era.

To the left of Case 4 (g): anta capital from the western porch of the Propylon of Ptolemy II with a relief group of two griffins devouring a stag. Thasian marble. (Fig. 57; see above, p. 96. 285-281 B.C.). On permanent loan from the Louvre.

Fig. 57. Anta Capital from the Propylon of Ptolemy II. 285-281 B.C.

Case 4 contains fragments of sculpture.

Top shelf, left and right sections: fragments of sculptured lids from the coffered ceiling of the Propylon to the Hall of Choral Dancers, seemingly representations of certain divinities or heroes honored in the Sanctuary (Fig. 58). *ca.* 340 B.C.

Center: marble head from a small statue of a woman. *ca.* 350 B.C.

Second shelf, left section: fragments of marble statuettes dedicated in the Sanctuary and dating from the fourth to the first centuries B.C. At right, a female portrait head, perhaps

Fig. 58. Fragmentary Coffer Lid from the Hall of Choral Dancers (by Skopas?). *ca.* 340 B.C.

131

Photo Anna Wachsmann.
Fig. 59. Terracotta Head. *ca.* 510 B.C.

Queen Arsinoe III; in the background, the lower part of a large female statuette from the later fourth century B.C.

Center: fragments of bronze sculptures dedicated in the Sanctuary, including a marble eye and a copper eye-lid, once inserted into the faces of Greek bronze statues, along with a fragment of hair from another such work; a fragment of a wing; another of a club from a figurine of Herakles; a finger of a colossal statue, found in the Anaktoron; fragments of beard, finger, and serpent, possibly from the same statue; tassel; leaf. Bronze statuette of Herakles with lion's skin, club, and kantharos, fourth century B.C.

Right section: terracotta figurines and fragments from various sites. In the background: to the right, a large, fragmentary female head of Ionic style from a head vase (Attic) (Fig. 59), *ca.* 510 B.C.; to the left, statuette of a young seated shepherd with his dog at his right and his crook at his left, a Phrygian cap on his head (Attis?, from an unexcavated ancient site west of Chora), third century B.C. To the right, two draped figurines, missing their heads but preserving parts of their original brilliant coloring, from the foundation

132

level of the Doric marble building of the Kings of Macedon, fourth century before 317 B.C. (for the Doric building, see above, pp. 100ff.). Other fragments, perhaps from dedications.

Third shelf, left section: lower half of a large marble statuette of a woman (Victory?), *ca.* 450-440 B.C.; torso of a female statuette, Hellenistic; forelegs of a horse from a high relief, second century after Christ; the foot of a statuette (Pan or a satyr?). Two more fragmentary feet are from the pedimental sculptures of the Hieron, *ca.* 150-125 B.C.

Center and right sections: fragments of high reliefs representing centaurs and a low foliate relief from the ceiling of the pronaos of the Hieron (150-125 B.C.; other fragments, some of them restored to one slab, are in Vienna). At extreme right, elbow of a male figure.

Bottom shelf, from left to right: leg from a life-sized statue of a kouros, from the Sanctuary, sixth century B.C.; arm of a colossal male statue, from the Sanctuary, fifth century B.C.; draped leg and foot of a seated figure from a high relief, found in the Sanctuary; fragmentary votive relief representing two goddesses (Demeter and Persephone?), third century B.C.; fragmentary corner block from the frieze of dancers from the Hall of Choral Dancers, of which other parts are shown in this hall (Fig. 33, pp. 73f., 123f.).

Hall C

Opposite the entrance (a), a bench rests on two marble bench supports probably of the Early Imperial period, from the Sacristy (see above, pp. 61f.).

From here one sees, in the center of the room (b), a marble bench support ornamented on both sides, which stands in a base, found near the Hall of Choral Dancers (see above, p. 78). Late Hellenistic.

In the background (c) stands an akroterial statue of

Photo Anna Wachsmann.
Fig. 60. Marble Akroterial Figure of Victory from the Hieron.
150-125 B.C.

Victory from a rear corner of the Hieron (Fig. 60). The life-sized figure carved in Thasian marble fell in an earthquake in the early Imperial age and was replaced by a similar statue now in Vienna. In 1949, the broken pieces of the statue in Samothrace were found carefully buried along the western foundation of the Hieron. Four such figures crowned the four corners of the Hellenistic building.

The statue lacks the head, most of the right arm, the left hand, parts of the wings, and minor fragments. Nike once raised her right arm and gracefully poured a libation into a patera held in her left hand, as if she were an acolyte of the Great Gods (two fragmentary hands from companion figures, one holding a patera, the other the handle of her jug, are exhibited in Case 6 in this hall). She is clad in soft leather shoes, a chiton, and a cloak wrapped around the lower part of the body and the left arm. The prop on the right shoulder was barely visible in antiquity. It supported the wrist of the bent right arm. The once invisible back has cuttings for iron bars that held the figure in position. Traces of ancient repairs are visible in various places. The slender proportion of the torso is partly characteristic of the style of the period, partly the result of the high position in which the figure originally stood. The statue is of excellent workmanship of about 130 B.C. Additional fragments which could not be fitted on and fragments of the other akroterial Victories, including their Roman replacements, were found in the excavations but are not on exhibition.

Most of the cases in this hall contain finds from the Sanctuary; two cases and part of a third on the left contain objects found in tombs around the city. The description begins with the cases on the right of the entrance from Hall B.

Case 1, top shelf: handmade vases of the Bronze Age (second millennium B.C.) from a deposit of ceramics found accidentally in 1939 in Kariotes (Fig. 2, see above, p. 17; other fragmentary examples are in storage). In the center, a stone handle decorated with incised concentric circles (from the same period?) found near Chora; a small Stone Age flint implement found on the site of the ancient town.

Second shelf, left section, back: dark gray handmade bowls and cups of the pre-Greek inhabitants of Samothrace (Fig. 3), found in a sacrificial deposit on the site of the later Hall of Choral Dancers. First half of the seventh century B.C.; front: amphora stopper; lid handle; two fragments of large vessels with impressed decoration; center section: kantharos, kernos, and small lamp from Phonias, a city in the northern part of the island. Classical. Right section: imported and local pottery from a Peak Sanctuary near the Akropolis of the ancient city. Seventh century B.C. through the Hellenistic period.

Third shelf: wheel-made local Samothracian ceramics mostly of the seventh and sixth centuries B.C., often with plastic, incised, or punched decoration. In the center, a Corinthian alabastron with a sphinx and a swan.

Bottom shelf: large globular Archaic vessel with two horizontal handles (*kados*); a fragment of the upper part of a large amphora; at the right, restored upper part of a basin (lekane) with a horizontal glazed stripe on the outside and, on the glazed inside, the incised non-Greek word ΔΙΝ (see Case 11). Archaic period.

On top of the case, a restored one-handled pot (seventh-sixth centuries B.C.).

At the left, on a pedestal (d), a fragmentary Thasian marble reclining figure of a child from the left corner of the front pediment of the Hieron (see, also, Hall B, Case 4, and above, p. 82), *ca.* 150-125 B.C.

Case 2, first row: metal objects including, at the left, two gilded bronze letters from a relief inscription, on the façade, recording a restoration of the Hall of Votive Gifts. First

Photo James R. McCredie

Fig. 61. Gold Ornament. Achaemenid (slightly enlarged).

century B.C. (see above, p. 87). Beneath them, bronze decorations from doors and a ceiling; attribution to specific buildings uncertain.

Second row: bronze decorations mostly from the doors and ceiling of the Hieron, *ca.* 325 B.C. (see above, pp. 79ff.); furniture ornaments.

Third row: bronze jewelry chest found in the Sacristy; pieces of locks and a key; fragments of bronze vessels.

Fourth row: fibulae, the upper ones Archaic and Classical, the one decorated with a bird on a ring, first century after Christ; a bronze spatula; a lead and a bronze tack.

Fifth row: personal ornaments, including a gilded silver brooch of the Roman Imperial period in the shape of a pelta (Amazon shield); earrings; a Persian (Achaemenid) gold attachment in the shape of a lion with glass paste inlays (Fig. 61), fifth century B.C.; an embossed bronze plaque. Below a fragmentary miniature bone herm.

Sixth row: a fishhook (Fig. 15); two arrowheads; an inscribed lead sling bullet; fragments of an iron chain-mail corselet (Fig. 14), dating *ca.* 200 B.C.

Fig. 62. Subgeometric Kantharos. 700-650 B.C.

All the objects in the row and most of those in the third
to fifth rows are from votive gifts dedicated in the Sanctuary.

Case 3: Greek ceramic vessels and fragments from a
sacrificial deposit on the site of the later Hall of Choral Dancers (see also Case 1 and above, pp. 18, 40f., 175). First half
of seventh century B.C. Conceivably, this ware was produced
in Samothrace. Other such sherds have been found on Thasos, Lesbos, Lemnos, Chios, and in Troy.

The upper three shelves are occupied by restored vases
and fragments of a very fine ware with sparse, delicate glazed
ornamentation of "subgeometric" style, mostly huge kantharoi (Fig. 62), and Chiot and Corinthian fragments.

The lower shelf contains ceramics of local and Ionic manufacture.

Case 4: ceramics, mostly black-glazed, from the Sanctuary, sixth-fourth centuries B.C.

The three upper shelves show a selection of typical
vessels used in the feasts celebrated in connection with the
mysteries: drinking vessels in the form of kantharoi, skyphoi,
and sometimes kylikes and bowls with or without handles,
occasionally of small size. In the center of the third shelf, a
fish plate and two askoi (see above, pp. 41f. and Hall B, Case

1). The vases exhibited on the second and third shelves were all found in the Rotunda of Arsinoe in the earth fills brought in at the time of its construction (see above, pp. 62ff.).

Bottom shelf: upper parts of two inscribed amphorae; upper fragment of an Attic column krater, fifth century B.C.

Case 5: stamped and relief ceramics and fragments of glass.

In the right center, two fragments of a Thasian tripod decorated with two friezes in relief showing the Departure of Amphiaraos. Second quarter of the sixth century B.C. Beneath them, the bottom of a bowl decorated on the inside and under the foot with masks. Hellenistic period.

At the left center, stamped amphora handles. The upper five are from Loutra. The first three are stamped with symbols of the Great Gods: ΘΕΩΝ, kerykeion and ram's head, and kerykeion. Hellenistic. At the left: fragments of relief ceramics from the Hellenistic age. Stamped bowls with palmette decoration, fourth century B.C., and a terracotta appliqué in the form of a sphinx.

At the right, fragments of blown, molded, and cut glass vessels of the Roman Imperial period; glass ring stones and beads; two blue glass ornaments in the form of masks. Hellenistic.

Case 6: Recent finds from the Sanctuary are temporarily exhibited in the center and upper right sections of the top shelf. They include a feather from a wing of the Victory of Samothrace and the left hand that may have belonged to that statue.

Top shelf, left section: two marble hands, one holding a patera and the other the handle of a vessel which has broken away. These are from the northwestern akroterion of the Hieron and were similar to the hands once present on the southwestern akroterial statue in this hall (see above, p. 133ff.). *ca.* 130 B.C.

Shelves 2-4: in the center, oil lamps found in the Sanctuary and used in the nocturnal rites of the mysteries (see above, pp. 40ff.). The upper shelves show clay lamps in chronological order, from top to bottom, dating from the sixth century B.C. (Fig. 17) to the fourth century after Christ; two spouts of fifth-century lamps manufactured for use in the Sanctuary and stamped with the monogram ΘΕ alluding to the Great Gods. The lamps exhibited on the third shelf are the latest and were found standing on the floor of the Sacristy, where they were abandoned when the pagan cult ceased (see above, p. 62). To the left of them, a late antique relief lamp decorated with a bust with bow and quiver (Artemis?). Below, marble lamps (Fig. 16) and fragments of such lamps dating from the seventh (at the right) through the fourth centuries B.C., some of the later examples preserving on the rims parts of inscriptions "(property) of the Gods".

In the lateral sections, clay vessels from the Sanctuary. Some of those on the left date from the Hellenistic period, the rest from the Roman Imperial period. At the lower left, the upper part of an amphora; at the right, a cooking pot of the third-fourth centuries A.D.

Cases 7 and 8: the two lower shelves of Case 7 contain changing exhibits of various objects from the nekropoleis. On the two upper shelves, in the center of the third shelf, and in table Case 8 are fragments of figured Attic kraters from the debris of a burned structure which seems to have been devoted to drinking and eating. It is possible that this was in connection with the rites in the Sanctuary; the Attic pots are not only of high quality and unusually large size, but they were carefully preserved in the building, the oldest (*ca.* 540 B.C.) for well over two hundred years. The burned wreckage of the structure was used for fill, much of it in the area to the east of the Stoa, and it is not yet known where the building stood.

Case 7, top shelf, left section: the lower part of a large black-figured Attic column krater, attributed to the Painter of Louvre F6. The scenes show the departure of a hoplite seen off by standing men and women and figures in the presence of two seated sphinxes. Fragments of some figures are in the left portion of the center section. *ca.* 540 B.C.

Right section: fragmentary rim and neck of a large black-figured Attic column krater signed by a previously unrecorded potter Fεχεκλείδης and attributed to the Princeton Painter. The scenes showed the combat between Herakles and Kyknos in the presence of divinities, and Herakles and Athena journeying in a chariot attended by a Victory. Some fragments of the scenes are in the right portion of the central section. *ca.* 540 B.C.

Second shelf, left and right sections: fragments of a large Attic red-figured bell krater. The scene is the reception of Herakles among the gods of Olympos. The names of the divinities are painted next to their figures. *ca.* 415-400 B.C. (Fig. 63).

In the center, fragments of a red-figured Attic volute krater, with Ariadne beside the reclining Dionysos who is surrounded by his followers and theatrical figures. *ca.* 400 B.C.

Photo James R. McCredie
Fig. 63. Fragments of an Attic Red-Figured Bell Krater. *ca.* 415-400 B.C.

Photo James R. McCredie
Fig. 64. Fragments of
a Red-Figured Krater.
ca. 470-460 B.C.

Third shelf, center section: fragments of a large red-figured bell krater attributed to the Attic painter Hermonax. The scene showed a drinking party (symposion). The rim fragments with an ivy wreath on the top surface may have belonged to this krater. *ca.* 470-460 B.C.

On the tops of Cases 6 and 7: large vases used as ash urns in Archaic burials in the Southern Nekropolis.

Case 8: fragments of a huge red-figured Attic column (?) krater, signed by one Erasinos (otherwise unknown) as potter and decorated by an unidentified painter. The scene shows a group of warriors preparing for battle. The figured fragments are arranged to suggest their probable original relationship. At the front of the case are rim and handle fragments which may belong to the krater. *ca.* 470-460 B.C. (Fig. 64).

On a base between Cases 8 and 9 (e): fragment of a very large Archaic basin found in the Sanctuary.

Case 9: early Roman tomb material characterized by many figurines, ceramic unguent bottles, and a small number of glass vessels, most of them shaped by methods in use before the invention of glass blowing.

Top shelf, left section: objects from a tomb near the road along the seashore, including three fragments of ceramic jugs shaped like heads; two terracotta cocks; two vases of multi-colored sandcore glass, one with gold leaf embedded in a layer of transparent glass.

Center section: three terracottas from a tomb: a seated woman, a rooster, and a jug in the shape of a Negro head.

Center and right sections: objects from a burial of the Augustan period: two statuettes of draped boys; three small cooking pots, one with a perforated dish overturned on it; a cylindrical ceramic box (pyxis); and a brown glass bowl.

Second shelf, left section: tomb group comprising two terracotta statuettes of seated nude women; terracotta figurines of a bull and a dog; two small clay bottles; two mold-pressed glass bowls; a head-shaped jug of a boy wearing an unusual, possibly ritual, headdress (replicas from the same mold are at the left of the upper shelf and in the central section of this shelf).

Center section: replica of the head vase of the child in an unusual headdress back to back with another head jug of a

Photo Elsbeth B. Dusenbery
Fig. 65. Head Vase of a Youth. Augustan.

young man with long curling hair and strongly curved nose (Fig. 65). To right, two tomb groups. One with a terracotta group showing two youths unveiling an amphora; a terracotta figurine of a child dressed as a pantomime performer; two unguentaria, one clay, one blown glass; three glass astragals and game counters. The second group includes a large cylindrical pyxis.

Right section: two tomb groups, one containing a jug with applied molded decoration, the other including a head jug of a youth wearing a garland; a large bronze needle; and a lamp.

Third shelf, left section: eight glass vessels, seven blown and one core-molded, found together in a Roman cremation burial in the storage jar exhibited beneath them on the bottom shelf.

Center section: objects, including a sandcore glass amphoriskos, a ceramic pyxis, and various vases, all from an inhumation burial. (The jewelry at the lower right in Case 4 in Hall D belongs to this group.) The tomb was that of a young woman and a baby whose bones were found in the big jug exhibited here in the central section of the bottom shelf.

Right section: a terracotta statuette of a seated nude woman wearing boots, and a ceramic head of a boy with braided hair, both probably from the same workshop, although they were not found together. Other objects from a deposit in the Southern Nekropolis, including a large terracotta draped female figure; the head of a similar statuette; a terracotta rooster; and two sandcore glass flasks.

Bottom shelf, right section: a storage pot typical of those used for Roman cremation burials; center: a blue glass bottle deformed in a pyre.

Case 10: contains chiefly later Roman tomb material, generally characterized by plentiful blown glass, egg-shell thin ceramic cups and delicate bone and glass toilet implements.

Photo Anna Wachsmann.
Fig. 66. Terracotta Statuette
from the South Nekropolis.
Third Century B.C.

Ceramic unguentaria and terracotta figurines are rare in the later graves.

Top shelf, left section and left part of center section: a glass aryballos, tumblers and flasks from various tombs, a glass button, two bone buttons, and a round bone box.

Center right and right section: objects from two burials, one of the first half of the third century B.C. and one of the last quarter of the first century B.C. The diggers of the later grave partially disturbed the earlier one, and one figurine of

Photo Elsbeth B. Dusenbery
Fig. 67. Glass Jug. Early Imperial.

a draped woman from the earlier group found its way into the later burial. Three draped figurines (the largest, Fig. 66) and a New Comedy head from the earlier group are at the back of this section. From the later group come the twin figurines of boys in cloaks, four figurines of seated nude women (Fig. 10), small pots, blown glass bottle, glass bowl, bone box. The tallest female figure (Fig. 66) and the Comedy head are not contemporary with the rest, but were apparently retained in the pithos from an original burial of the early third century B.C.

Second shelf, left section: gifts from an inhumation burial, including silver earrings; glass and bone hairpins; finely carved round bone pyxides; a bone spoon; an egg-shell thin red clay bowl; a square glass jug (Fig. 67); a tumbler; small flasks.

Center section: contents of a tomb containing a bronze stylus; a bronze needle; a fragmentary bronze brooch in the shape of an Amazon shield (pelta); glass flasks; knucklebones; a bone pyxis; a bone spoon; a ceramic bowl on a foot decorated with molded reliefs and originally covered with yellow lead glaze probably intended to imitate gold, *ca.* 10-20 A.D.

Right section: glass vessels from various graves; two small bottles at center right with a globular jug found with them.

Third shelf, left section: a glass beaker (Fig. 68); a bronze hairpin; three egg-shell thin ceramic cups; the lid of the Roman storage jar shown beneath it on the lower shelf. These are finds from a (family?) burial which included five cremations and one inhumation, all approximately contemporary. First half of the first century after Christ. The glass tumbler was found inside the jar on the bottom shelf.

Center and right sections: the contents of a Roman chamber tomb containing four skeletons, found in 1952 along the road at the seashore beneath the western hill of the ancient town. This group included a number of glass vessels; a *terra sigillata bowl*; an iron strigil; a bronze mirror; ivory pins, two of them finely carved; ring-handled hairpins; an embossed gold diadem with the rayed head of the Sun God flanked by Victories driving chariots; gold foil leaves from a funerary crown and its probable central element, a gold disk with the impression of an Anatolian coin representing the heroized Antinous. *ca.* 135 A.D.

Bottom shelf, left and center sections: two Roman storage jars which were used for cremation burials.

Photo Elsbeth B. Dusenbery
Fig. 68. Glass Beaker. Early Imperial.

Fig. 69. Limestone Inscription in Pre-Greek Language.
Fourth Century B.C.

Right section: a group of pottery vessels from various tombs, including a small mortar with pestle in the form of a dog's head; cylindrical box made of lead.

Displayed along the walls of the hall are a few large vases found in the nekropoleis. They include wine amphorae of the fifth and fourth centuries B.C., imported from various Greek cities, and a large Roman storage jar.

Photo Anna Wachsmann
Fig. 70. Graffito in Pre-Greek Language on the Lip of a Kylix.

Case 11: inscriptions.

In the center: a fragmentary limestone stele (Fig. 69) with the right part of a long inscription in Greek letters but of the pre-Greek, probably Thracian, language spoken by the natives of Samothrace and still used in the liturgy of the cult in the first century B.C. (see above, pp. 18, 30ff.). *ca.* 400 B.C.

At the left: fragments of vases with inscriptions in the same non-Greek language. Sixth to fourth centuries B.C. (Fig. 70; see above, pp. 18, 30ff. and also Case 1, lower right).

At the right: fragments of incised and stamped pottery found in the Sanctuary. They mainly show Θ or ΘΕ as abbreviations of "The Gods"; on one, the crossbar of the epsilon is formed by a kerykeion, the symbol of Hermes Kadmilos. The bowl on the lower right is stamped (Fig. 71) with the full word ΘΕΩΝ "(property) of the Gods". The stamped items were from vessels and lamps manufactured for use in the Sanctuary. Above, in the center, an invocation to "the boy" (ΠΑΙ). At the left, a fragment of an inscribed pipe of the sixth century B.C. from the sacrificial area later included in the Altar Court (see above, p. 89). Below, a fragmentary dish with incised letters scratched out after ritual use (see

Fig. 71. Detail of a Hellenistic Bowl Stamped Θεῶν
(slightly enlarged).

above, p. 41). Sixth to second centuries B.C.

Case 12, top shelf: bronzes of the Christian period. From left to right: arm of Byzantine balance scale and a weight with incised cross and letters; three Byzantine coins; a bronze cross; a buckle and a fragment of a Byzantine votive cross with the incised head of a saint; a key; an arrowhead; a door-knocker(?); a fragment of a circular Byzantine candelabrum (polycandelon) from the church near the ancient harbor.

Second shelf: at the left, fragments of Byzantine glazed pottery; a stamped tile; a clay stamp for bread brought to the church as an offering bearing the inscription ΑΠΟΔ[οσις(?)] (nowadays such stamps are usually made of wood). At the right, fragments of medieval pottery.

Third shelf: fragments of ancient stucco. At the left, from the Altar Court (see above, p. 89) and the Hieron (see above, p. 83); at the right, from the Anaktoron (see above, p. 58) and the Hall of Votive Gifts (see above p. 87); at the front, from the Stoa (see above, p. 107). Sixth century B.C. to third century after Christ.

Bottom shelf: a large marble plane (float) used to smooth

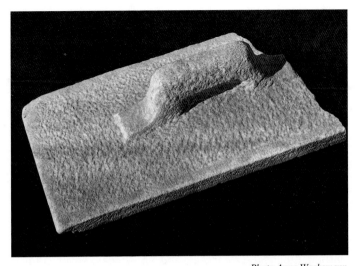

Photo Anna Wachsmann

Fig. 72. Fragmentary Marble Float Found in the Hall of Votive Gifts.

coats of stucco, found broken and abandoned by a late-antique workman on the stucco floor of the Hall of Votive Gifts (Fig. 72, see above, p. 87). Fourth century after Christ. In the center, a modern wooden implement of the same type now used in Samothrace. At the right, a fragmentary marble relief (Early Christian; seventh century after Christ?).

On top of this case: a large Byzantine bronze vessel.

Hall D

Finds from the nekropoleis, ultimately to be installed in Hall E, are provisionally exhibited in this hall. It is dominated by a cast of the famous statue known as the Victory of Samothrace found in the Sanctuary in 1863 and now in the Louvre in Paris (a). The cast is a gift of the French Government. To the right, photographs of the statue on its ship's-prow base and of its fragmentary right hand, discovered in 1950, and also on exhibition in the Louvre.

For the Nike Monument, see above, pp. 102ff.

Opposite this cast against the western wall:

Case 1: contains vases imported from Athens during the sixth and fifth centuries B.C. and used as containers for cremation burials in the nekropoleis.

Top shelf, at the left: three small drinking cups and a miniature hydria from a cremation burial of *ca.* 500-490 B.C. The large black-figured pelike on a pedestal to the left of this case (b) was the principal vase of this burial; it is attributed to the Eucharides Painter and shows scenes of pressing and drinking new wine, with Herakles and Dionysos participating. Silver earrings and an Archaic silver coin of Akanthos found inside the pelike with the ashes are exhibited in Case 4 together with other precious jewelry from various graves.

Center and right sections: a red-figured hydria of the late fifth century B.C. and a black-figured amphora of the early fifth century B.C. with the small vases found with them.

Second shelf, left to right: a black-figured amphora with a black-glazed cup that was used to cap it; another black-glazed cup used as a cap (principal vessel not on exhibition); black-figured pelike attributed to the Eucharides Painter with scenes of music-making on both sides (Fig. 73), *ca.* 500-490 B.C.

Right section: a red-figured amphora, probably by the painter Hermonax, *ca.* 470-460 B.C., with a cup and a small olpe found with it. A wine amphora from this burial is exhibited on the left balustrade of the stairway leading to Hall A (d).

Third shelf, left to right: a red-figured pelike showing a satyr and a maenad, together with its cap, a stemmed plate; a large black-glazed oinochoe with a round mouth, found with

Fig. 73. Black-Figured Pelike. Late Archaic.

the one-handled cup shown with it; a red-figured pelike with conversation scenes.

Bottom shelf, left section: the lower part of a black-figured amphora of the late sixth century B.C. which had been cut in half before its use as a burial vessel. On one side, two horsemen in Thracian cloaks rearing over a fallen warrior; on the other, a procession of warriors.

Center section: a red-figured water jar (kalpis).

Right section: a red-figured pelike with a satyr and a maenad on the principal panel and two conversing figures on the reverse. A few unrelated dishes are also exhibited on this shelf.

On top of this case is a Panathenaic amphora attributed to the Euphiletos Painter or his workshop, *ca.* 525 B.C., with armed Athena on the obverse and a footrace on the reverse.

Case 2: contains Archaic vessels used as ash urns, many with the cups that capped them. Here, in contrast with Case 1, the vases are not from Athens, although some of the cups which capped them are, but from other regions of the Archaic Greek world, including Lemnos and Asia Minor. Some of the otherwise unknown fabrics may be Samothracian. Decorations on many of these pots have been severely damaged or lost through the adverse effects of burial.

Top shelf, at the left: a Samothracian (?) amphora once decorated with horses' heads in panels.

Center section: an amphora of the type called Clazomenian with a round hole cut in its body, one of a number of pots found with this unexplained feature; and two lekanides.

Right section: a small, round-mouthed jug of a commonly found local type with its capping cup in place; a flat-bottomed drinking cup of rare form (karchesion, Fig. 74).

Second shelf, left to right: an amphora with a round hole cut in it, together with its egg-shell thin Attic skyphos cap; an

Photo James R. McCredie
Fig. 74. Samothracian Karchesion. Early Archaic.

154

Fig. 75. Covered Jar Imported from Lemnos. Sixth Century B.C.

amphora, probably Samothracian, with a sharp ridge below the rim and a lion in black paint on the body; an Attic cup found with the lion amphora; a small pitcher with an ancient repair; a covered jar imported from Lemnos (Fig. 75).

Third shelf, left to right: a red clay amphora, probably made in Samothrace, which was once decorated but has lost its paint, and an Attic cup possibly related to it; a scale-decorated amphora, probably also made locally; two East Greek amphorae, one of unknown fabric, one of "Clazomenian" type decorated with winged horses.

Bottom shelf, left and center sections: amphorae with scale and horse-protome decorations (Samothracian?); an Archaic Attic cup.

Right section: a stamnos with maeander pattern from Lemnos, of a type generally dated in the seventh century B.C.; the lid of a similar Lemnian vessel.

Case 3: contains various ceramics and tomb groups from the nekropoleis, most of them dating from the fifth century B.C.

Top shelf, left section: a restored Attic jug with a trefoil mouth whose fragments were found inside the wine am-

Fig. 76. Ceramic Basket. Fourth Century B.C.

phora exhibited on the right balustrade of the steps leading to Hall A; a small vase in the shape of an almond found with the adjacent red-figured lekythos and the group of tiny objects, including a yellow glass bead and a miniature double ax of bronze. At the back of the shelf: two lekythoi; a black-glazed baby feeder.

Center section: objects from the tomb of a child including a terracotta figurine of a seated woman; a baby feeder; a miniature basket (Fig. 76). Early fourth century B.C.

Right section: tomb group consisting of an askos, a lekythos, and an iron strigil, late fifth century B.C.; a fragment of a clay bottle in the shape of a fat man, sixth century B.C.; two sandcore glass aryballoi, and a salt cellar, early fifth century B.C.

Second shelf, left and center sections: some vases from a group found together, including a partly red-glazed cup; a red-figured Attic pelike; a locally made jar utilizing a black-glazed lid from an Attic vessel.

Right section: fragments of Attic figured vases used in burial ceremonies and purposely broken.

Third shelf, left and center sections: a gray amphora with its matching lid; an Attic one-handler; a black-figured Attic amphora of the sixth century B.C.

Right section: a red-figured Attic amphora, *ca.* 470-460 B.C., with the striped cup used to cap it and four silver earrings and a linked silver ring and dress pin (fibula) found inside.

Bottom shelf: various ceramics, probably locally made.

On top of the case, a large locally made jug from a cremation burial.

To the right of the steps leading to Hall A, on the floor (c): a terracotta sarcophagus of the early fifth century B.C. Probably made for a child, it was reused for an adult burial in the late first or early second century A.D., when one end was broken away (now restored in plaster) to accommodate a longer body. Some fragments of the missing half of the lid indicate that it was flat. On the balustrade (d): an imported amphora, possibly Attic, found with a jug with trefoil mouth (in Case 3, at the left of the upper shelf). *ca.* 460 B.C.

Case 4: contains most of the precious jewelry and silver coins found in the nekropoleis.

Left section: above, groups of silver jewelry, including four earrings (one severely burned), a chain, and a fibula, of the late sixth or early fifth century B.C. Below, a fibula, silver earring, and coin from the cremation burial in the large black-figured pelike on the pedestal to the left of Case 1. To the left, two gold lion's-head earrings, a silver coin of Philip II of Macedon, and a group of tiny gold beads from a grave of the fourth century B.C. Nearby, two flat pendant ornaments of gold foil from a destroyed tomb; a gold ring, a single gold lion's-head earring, and a silver coin of Maroneia from a burial of the late fourth century B.C. Below, suite of gold jewelry including ring, earrings, necklace, and crown from the tomb of a little girl, third century B.C.

Center section: on a plaque, elements of funerary crowns, chiefly leaves made of gold foil. The two principal sets of

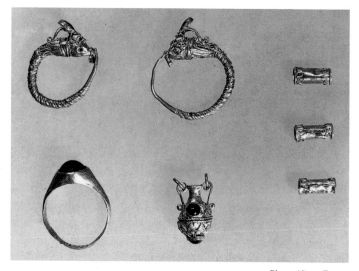

Photo Alison Frantz

Fig. 77. Gold Jewelry from a Late Hellenistic Tile Tomb.

leaves are from a tomb rich in terracottas (Case 5, second shelf). The other leaves, diamond shapes, and rosettes are from various burials. Below to the left, gold earring with winged Eros from a burial of the third century B.C.; a round earring with filigree decoration of the late fourth century B.C. In the center, five silver coins from the Southern Nekropolis, including coins of Teos and Akanthos and two Classical coins of Samothrace with helmeted heads. At the right, a gold ring with glass stone and a cylindrical gold bead with thunderbolt pattern in filigree wire.

Right section: at top, a gold ring, earrings, silver spoon, and gold foil leaves of a crown from a burial of the Augustan era (see Hall C, Case 9, third shelf, for pottery and glass from this tomb). Below, a large gold-foil-covered earring with two glass beads ornamenting it, from another Augustan burial; silver jewelry from various tombs of the early Roman period. Below, gold earrings, ring, and pendant, all set with garnets, gold-foil oak leaves and coin impression from a funerary crown, tubular gold beads and glass beads, all from a burial of the early first century B.C. (Fig. 77; for pottery from this tomb, see Case 5, third shelf, right section).

Case 5: contains objects from burials of the fourth century B.C. and the Hellenistic period.

Top shelf, left section: examples of kantharoi of the fourth and third centuries B.C. found associated with various tombs (Fig. 18).

Center section: three terracotta figurines of boys wrapped in cloaks and wearing beret-like caps; behind them, pottery of the early third century B.C. found associated with them.

Right section: a terracotta figurine of a seated boy wearing a cloak and a beret; examples of drinking cups of the fourth and third centuries B.C. from various burials; an iron ring, perhaps belonging to an initiate in the cult of the Great Gods (see above, p. 30, Fig. 9); head of a terracotta statuette of a youth with long hair.

Second shelf: devoted to the contents of a pithos used as a burial container for two young people. Probably third century B.C.

Left section: four of five replicas of a terracotta group found in this tomb; two are fragmentary (the fifth was too shattered to be repaired). The group shows a winged boy playing a cithara being followed and embraced by a nude baby (Eros and Adonis? Fig. 78). Background: terracotta group of two winged boys raising a large krater (thymiaterion). At the front: thirty-three glass counters, probably for use in a game; four of the seventy-six knucklebones found in this burial, two perforated and two inscribed with letters.

Center section: figurine of a flying Eros of fine quality (Fig. 79). At the left, a replica of the flying figure, less completely preserved. At the right, a right arm from a third fig-

Photo Alison Frantz
Fig. 78. Terracotta Group.
Third Century B.C.

ure of this type, showing that, in the best preserved example, the forearm between the elbow and the hand was omitted by an error of the coroplast; a hollow clay replica of an air-inflated ball.

Right section: a gold ring (gold-foil leaves of crowns from this tomb are displayed on the central plaque of Case 4); two grotesque heads from terracotta statuettes; a terracotta figurine of a satyr carrying a winged child on his back. At the back, a terracotta plaque showing a youth approaching an altar and a herm; some small vases found in the pithos.

Third shelf, left section: tomb group of the fourth century B.C. including a bronze mirror; a terracotta flower from a funerary crown (other elements unrestorable; compare restored portion of a similar crown, Case C6, left section); various vases.

Center section: small grave groups of the third century B.C. One included a small terracotta herm, a lamp, a kantharos, a molded askos. The other consists of two unguent

Photo Alison Frantz
Fig. 79. Terracotta Statuette of Eros. Third Century B.C.

jars and a glazed bowl incised with pentagons.

Right section: pottery vases, including a painted jar, a lamp and a Pergamene cup with molded erotic scenes, from a burial of the early first century B.C. (this grave included the splendid suite of gold and garnet jewelry exhibited at the lower left of Case C4).

Bottom shelf, left section: tomb group of the late second century B.C., including a molded bowl.

Center section: two cylindrical ceramic boxes, one very large and decorated with applied molded garlands. *ca.* first century B.C.

Right section: a group of vases, including a black-glazed pyxis, from a deposit in the Southern Nekropolis, probably of the third century B.C.

On top of this case: a large East Greek Archaic amphora decorated with scale pattern and palmettes, probably Samothracian.

Case 6: contains miscellaneous objects from burials and from the fills of the nekropoleis.

To the left: examples of the many bronze brooches (fibulae) found in the Southern Nekropolis, especially in the pyre areas; other ornaments and amulets, mostly of bronze; restored section of a funeral crown composed of terracotta berries and gilded bronze leaves on bronze stems, all mounted on a lead strip. Crowns of this type were found in a number of burials of the late fourth century B.C.

Left center, top to bottom: lid of a round bronze box; small bronze handles; a bronze mirror; a bronze strigil; a bronze hinge; a bronze fishhook; bronze tweezers; a bronze needle; a writing tool (stylus); a clay loom weight.

Right center, top to bottom: glass gaming pieces; glass and bone knucklebones; a fragment of a terracotta plaque with relief decoration of a knucklebone; an almond and a miniature pomegranate modeled in clay.

At right: fragments of bone hairpins; pieces of bone boxes; a fragmentary bone stylus in a case; bone and glass buttons; a bone reel of unknown use.

Study Collections

Inscriptions. In the portico of the courtyard, inscriptions are stored for the convenience of specialists. They include, in the east wing, marble decree stelai of the town of Samothrace, mostly of the Hellenistic age, once exhibited in the town in the Sanctuary of Athena; one fragmentary gray limestone stele of the fourth century B.C. in "Aeolic" dialect (see above, p. 19); inscriptions of the ambassadors to the Samothracian festivals from the Hellenistic period.

In the southeast corner of the courtyard (a) stands the inscribed base and the Doric capital of its supporting column of the monument of Philip V dedicated by the Macedonians to the Great Gods, found to the east of the Stoa. *ca.* 200 B.C. (Fig. 80; see above, pp. 106).

Along the southern part of the eastern wing and in the southern wing: catalogues of initiates, both Greek and Latin, dating from the Hellenistic and Roman ages.

In the western wing, inscriptions referring to buildings and tombstones are stored.

Photo James R. McCredie

Fig. 80. Capital and Inscribed Base of the Monument of Philip V.

In the intervals between the piers on the eastern side there are fragments of the dedicatory inscriptions of the Rotunda of Arsinoe and the Propylon of Ptolemy II and a dedication from an altar erected in honor of a king (Lysimachos?). In the southern intercolumniation of the eastern wing and in the southern wing there are inscriptions from honorary statues and dedications by private individuals.

On the southern wall (b) are fragments of the gutter of the Hieron with lion-headed waterspouts (see above, p. 82).

In the portico (c), there are also five large pithoi, one with a lead cover, which were used for burials in the western cemetery. These date from the fourth century B.C. A sixth, enormous pithos was found in the sea off Kamariotissa.

In the eastern wing and in the courtyard, remnants of the walls of a small Byzantine chapel are visible, as well as some medieval annexes, possibly of a monastery.

Other materials. All the finds from the American excavations not displayed in the museum are stored either in drawers in the museum cases or in storerooms. They can be made available to specialists by the excavators or the Museum authorities upon prior arrangement.

V

Excavations outside the Sanctuary of the Great Gods

The archaeological investigation of Samothrace outside the Sanctuary of the Great Gods which has, in recent years, been carried out by the 19th Ephoreia of Prehistoric and Classical Antiquities (Komotini), has provided important information about the cultural features of the island from the Neolithic period to Roman times. More especially, as regards the prehistoric and protohistoric past, the evidence allows us to form a first account of the course of the island's development from the appearance of the first organized Samothracian community to the Dark Ages, before the arrival of Greek settlers and the creation of the city-state.

At *Mikro Vouni,* on the southwest coast of Samothrace on the west bank of the torrent *Polypoudi,* rises the mound of the prehistoric settlement where the emergence of the complex society in Samothrace took place. Built on a promontory, it encompassed about 2-1/2 acres and can be seen as a typical example of a proto-urban "town" in the Aegean of the 3rd millennium B.C., with a population of the order of 400-600 individuals. A small bay to the southeast formed a natural harbor for the boats of that time and was clearly one of the main reasons for the choice of the site; in the broader environs of the latter lies nearly the whole of the agricultural land of Samothrace, with the best expanses for cultivation west of the present village of *Alonia,* which is currently the most important center of agricultural production. The excavation has, so far, concentrated on the cultural sequence of the site, as it is preserved in the excavated stratified deposits, which, on the summit of the mound (12.8 meters above sea level) have a depth of some 8 meters. The earliest phase of settlement is dated to the end of the 6th millennium B.C. and may be compared for its absolute chronology with the *Beşik-Sivritepe* horizon in the Troad, which is characterized by pattern-burnished ware, as well as with the first phase at Sitagroi and Dikili Tash in eastern Macedonia and with Paradimi I-II in western Thrace (Fig. 81). Radiocarbon dating shows that here, too, there is a gap in the last phase of Late Neolithic which, although not archaeologically detectable, divides the *ca.* 3-meter deep Neolithic layers from the earliest layers of the Bronze Age. If we compare the chronological series of the latter with the corresponding ones at Troy, we may be able to suppose some delay in the resettlement(?) of the site which took place *ca.* 2900 B.C., likely the result of the uncertainties of the insular environment (Fig. 82). The apparently earlier Neolithic sequences, at *Makri* (6th millennium) in Evros, 10 km. west of *Alexandroupolis*, and at *Hoca Çeşme* (second half of the 7th and 6th millennium) in the Evros delta, 5 km. east of *Ainos* and an equal distance from the present shore of the Aegean, offer two examples of contemporary Neolithic sequences in the Samothracian Peraea. These sequences precede the sequence at *Mikro Vouni*, which

Photo D. Matsas
Fig. 81. Mikro Vouni: Human-shaped Vase.
Second Half of the 5th Millenium B.C.

Photo D. Matsas

Fig. 82. Mikro Vouni: Terracotta Head. First Half of the
3rd Millenium B.C.

is their immediate successor. Although we are deprived of
adequate evidence, perhaps we can relate the end of the development of these sites in the Peraea with the settlement of
the island and the beginning of the sequence at *Mikro Vouni*,
at least to the extent to which it can be now tracked. As regards the relations of the late Neolithic sequence at *Mikro
Vouni* with the central Aegean, the sequence at *Pefkakia* in
Thessaly constitutes the nearest parallel. The pottery follows
the tradition of Aegean Thrace, known as the *Paradimi culture*, and has a perhaps genetic relationship with the ceramic
production of the Balkan hinterland, such as *Karanovo III*
and *Vinča* A. The northern ancestries of the late Neolithic
culture in Samothrace do not constitute an impediment to
relations with the rest of the Aegean world as well. The
settlement was abandoned in the advanced middle Bronze
Age, around 1700 B.C., when the pottery of its final phase
can be compared with that of early *Troy VI*, and it was never
inhabited again.

One of the most important discoveries of the archaeo-

Photo D. Matsas

Fig. 83. Mikro Vouni: Clay Sealing with the First Part of the
Hieroglyphic Libation Formula. 19th -18th Century B.C.

logical research at *Mikro Vouni* and more generally in the
northeast Aegean was that of some clay documents of a
Minoan (probably Knossian) archive from the middle Bronze
Age layers (19th-18th century B.C.), found for the first time
so far from Crete. The Minoan presence in Samothrace and
in the northeast Aegean, certainly a palace enterprise, had a
commercial character, and its main contents were metals.
One inscription in Linear A script is one of its earliest uses
outside Crete, while the sealings with the first part of the
hieroglyphic Libation Formula (hieroglyphic sign-syllabo-
grams of the double axe and sepia) perhaps underline the
role of religious ideas in the economic activities of the Minoan elite (Fig. 83). Both the double axe and the sepia (cut-
tlefish, which can be interpreted as a fish or an octopus, as
well) have been connected with the Kabeiroi, who in Samothrace are known as the Great Gods, and the Great Mother,
who constituted the central figure of their cult. It is very
likely that the root Ἀξι- of the names Axieros, Axiokersos,

and Axiokersa is connected with the double axe. The origin of the word Kabeiroi, who, in neighboring Lemnos, accompanied Hephaistos and were heavenly smiths, is unknown, but one interpretation connects it with the Sumerian *kabar*, which means copper. Perhaps, then, we may theorize that the introduction of their cult in Samothrace, as well as in Lemnos and Imbros, is related to the trade in metals which came here from the Black Sea at the end of the early and beginning of the middle Bronze Age period (Fig. 84).

If we should connect *Mikro Vouni* with the Pelasgians, whom Herodotus mentions as the oldest inhabitants of Samothrace, in the second great episode of the island's development, which marks its entrance into the Dark Age, a tribe of Thracian origin is involved. Already in 1928, Professor N. Andriotis, who was studying in Samothrace the linguistic idiom of the island's inhabitants, had remarked three mega-

Photo D. Matsas

Fig. 84. Mikro Vouni: Partial View of the Ruins of the Settlement. Second Half of the 3rd Millenium B.C.

169

lithic tombs of the early Iron Age at the site *Gialomandra*, on the northern slopes of the hill *Vrychos* northwest of *Chora* (Fig. 85). In 1986, in the course of road construction on the western slope of the hill, remains were found of a settlement which, as the study of its pottery shows, is of the same period. The systematic survey of the area led to the discovery of an extensive fortification wall with "Cyclopean" characteristics enclosing an oblong, relatively level area of *ca.* 2-1/4 acres on the crest of the ridge (elevation 340-370 m.). The site offers natural defense and access to water supplies. The wall, whose total length is about 850 m., encloses the flat summit and follows the contours of the ground. In general, its foundation rests on the rock, which often is incorporated in its construction, and in places the rock is so high and steep that it forms a natural wall. It is built of boulders of various sizes and irregular shapes, scarcely trimmed at all, forming two strong faces which enclose a loosely laid filling of rubble and small stones. In some places, depending on the shape of the ground and defensive requirements, it is built entirely of boulders, fitted together with inserted stones and pebbles (Fig. 86). In others, the line of the wall is shown by the extensive working of the rock, on which the first course of boulders rested. The width of the wall varies from 2.20 m. to 3.30 m. and in many places is 3.20 m. The fortification is divided into two main parts, the lower in the north (area *ca.* 1-3/4 acres) and the higher in the south (area 3/8 acre), divided by a crosswall which leaves a narrow communicating passage at the east. A lower leg at the southeast part of the circuit is fragmentary and encloses a sloping area of *ca.* 3/8 acre which forms two successive, relatively level terraces. Similar terraces were formed on the southwest, west and east slopes of the hill, where the terrain allowed it, with the clear purpose of accommodating habitation. Excavation at the north part, which has the advantage of natural fortification over the much larger southern part, did not reveal

Photo D. Matsas

Fig. 85. Gialomandra: Megalithic Tomb. 11th Century B.C.

permanent structures in the thin deposit which covered the natural rock. The only exception is a circular(?) structure, a part of the foundation of which, built of one course of stones, was uncovered at the northeast corner. Circular constructions are known from the akropolis of *Ergani* (*Asar Tepe*) inland from the Thracian coast opposite Samothrace, a site which is also related to *Vrychos* in its two-part division. If the hypothesis that the southern and northern parts of the fortification were intended as refuges for the local population and their livestock respectively is correct, the constructions in the former must have been temporary and of perishable materials. As survey shows, the houses of the settlement were scattered over the slopes of the hill, where the contours of the ground permitted. This settlement pattern is completely different from that seen at *Mikro Vouni*, with its nucleated, proto-urban habitation, and it is indicative of a society employed exclusively(?) in stock breeding (in spite of the fact that no animal bones were found in the limited

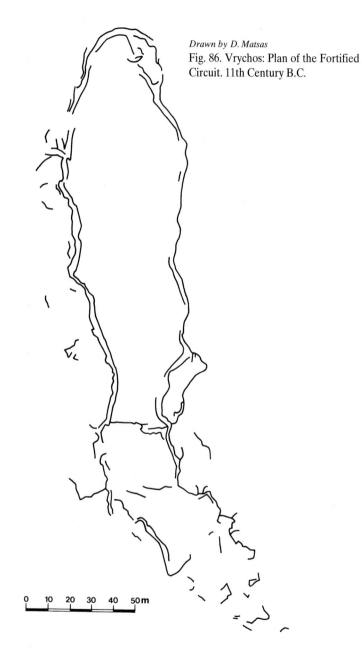

Drawn by D. Matsas

Fig. 86. Vrychos: Plan of the Fortified Circuit. 11th Century B.C.

0 10 20 30 40 50 m

area excavated). The choice of the site, close to the village of *Chora*, under whose houses part of the Early Iron Age settlement may be found, must have been dictated by conditions similar to those which forced the medieval population of the island from the coast to the interior and to exactly the same place. The decoration of the pottery, which is nearly the only category of finds, is related especially to *Babadag I* group of the eastern Balkans. It can be dated in the 11th century B.C. and placed a little earlier than the pottery of *Troy VIIb2*. Material corresponding with that of *Vrychos* has been located in the coastal zone of the Samothracian Peraea, and, on the basis of these ceramics, perhaps we can speak of the use of the sea route in the migration of Thracian tribes related to it from the western shore of the Black Sea to the northeast Aegean. Vrychos perhaps formed the central fortification between two satellites, notably smaller circuits of the same time, which are located on the hills *Avgerinos* to the northeast and *Agianemi* to the southeast at a distance of 1 and 2 km. respectively.

In addition to *Mikro Vouni* and *Vrychos*, which form key sites for the study of the prehistory and protohistory of Samothrace, recent archaeological investigation in the Ancient City (*Palaiopoli*), at *Keramidaria*, and at *Mandal' Panagia* have begun to enrich our knowledge of the island in historical times. The plan of the ancient city of Samothrace, whose walls constitute one of the most striking examples of ancient Greek enceintes, is unknown owing to the lack of systematic investigation. Besides the systematic excavation of two of its cemeteries, the Northern and Southern Nekropoleis, outside the west leg of the walls by the American excavators of the Sanctuary (pp. 91ff), the more recent salvage excavation of the Greek Archaeological Service in the Northern Nekropolis (Fig. 87) and older small-scale excavations, recent (1995) trial excavation on a small, flat terrace,

Photo Ch. Karadima

Fig. 87. North Nekropolis: Terracotta Statuette of a Dancer.
Middle 4th Century B.C.

Fig. 88. Keramidaria: Pottery Kiln. Roman Period.

strewn with marble fragments on the slope a short distance
southeast of the Gattilusi towers, where the ruins of the
chapel of *Aï-Giorgi* stand, unearthed a mass of broken architectural members which come from at least two buildings
(4th to 3rd century B.C.), one Doric and one Ionic. Notable
among them are pieces of a Doric epistyle with regula and
guttae, part of a frieze of triglyphs and metopes, parts of an
Ionic epistyle with an astragal moulding between two fasciae
and a Lesbian cyma crown, simas (one of which is ornamented with a rinceau) with lion's-head spouts, bases and
drums of Ionic columns, and marble Corinthian cover-tiles.
In addition to a small amount of Classical and Hellenistic
pottery, many sherds of sub-Geometric kantharoi and amphorae of G 2-3 ware recovered, dated in the first half of the
seventh century B.C. and similar to those from the Hall of
Choral Dancers in the Sanctuary of the Great Gods. Three
large rectangular blocks were found *in situ* and must belong

Photo Ch. Karadima
Fig. 89. Keramidaria: Stamped Amphora Handle. End of the 4th - First Half of the 3rd Century B.C.

to the foundation of a large building. A mosaic floor of marble chips which covers much of the area around the ruined chapel of *Aï-Giorgi* belongs to another large building of still uncertain date. The completion of the excavation will, we hope, give us more information about the buildings that stood there.

The north coastal road, after the turnings for the villages of *Kato* and *Pano Kariotes*, brings us to the site *Keramidaria*, 5 km. east of *Palaiapoli*, where there were discovered at least two workshops for the production of Hellenistic amphorae. The extensive complex of ceramic workshops to which they belong already was known in the 1970s after the works to open the road, which cut through it. Excavation of the area in 1989, 1991 and 1996 brought to light south of the road a large, rectangular manufacturing area, investigated in the neighboring area, north of the road toward the sea, a waster dump from an older workshop, and uncovered three kilns on the shore *ca.* 500 m. to the east (Fig. 88). The rectangular manufacturing area, 6.50 by 20.30 m., connected with pre-firing manufacturing process, was in use in late Hellenistic and early Roman times. The excavation of the waster-dump produced a considerable number of stamped handles (*ca.* 2000) and fragments of amphoras which represented *ca.*

176

85% of the discarded material. At least 70 types of different stamps have been recognized, which, as a rule are rectangular in shape, but in some cases circular or oval. They are stamped with symbols similar to those from other centers of amphora production, which refer to the maker and the workshop. Among the symbols are some which also appear on the coinage of the city of Samothrace and which appear to have a special connection with the Sanctuary and the cult of the Great Gods/Kabeiroi (kerykeion, ram's head, cap, star, dolphin, etc.). Usually there is also a name (*Simon, Prokles, Agathon*) often in the genitive case (*Theondou, Phertatou, Philonidou*). The names on the stamps most likely refer to some annual official, a sort of Eponymous who exercised some sort of control over finance (taxation?) (Fig. 89). On the basis of the dated stamps and typology of the amphoras, we can place the functioning of the workshop for the production of amphoras with stamped handles in the second half of the 4th and in the 3rd century B.C. This period is marked not only by the great flowering of the Sanctuary of the Great Gods which saw not only an unprecedented architectural development but also a spread of the Samothracian Gods to sites far from the island owing to the rise in popularity of the mysteries. Perhaps the spread of Samothracian amphorae and their contents, most likely wine, to cities of the Thracian coast (*Amphipolis, Abdera, Maroneia, Zone, Doriskos*), of the Northeast Aegean (*Thasos of Lesbos*), and of the Black Sea (*Odessos, Bizone, Kallatis, Olbia*) as well as to the Balkan interior (*Kabyle, Seuthopolis*) is to be tied to this spread of the Gods and their mysteries. Finally, *ca.* 500 m. east of the rectangular manufacturing area and the waster dump, excavation brought to light three kilns, one next to the other and in a very good state of preservation, which must have formed part of a larger complex of kilns. They were constructed on the waster dump of an earlier amphora workshop and date in Imperial times. They belong to the type of the vertical kiln with rectangular plan, supported above a central corridor and with a pillar engaged in the rear wall. The excavation is not yet complete.

At the site *Mandal' Panagia*, on a foothill of the peak *Ai-Lias*, which descends in a northwesterly direction to the torrent Xeropotamo, between elevations 370 and 390 m. and *ca.* 250 m. from the chapel of that name, is located a sanctuary probably of a female divinity. The archaeological site was discovered by the Samothracian scholar N. Phardys (1855-1901). Among the objects of Phardys' collection, first described by O. Kern in 1893, female terracotta figurines are very numerous, like "the archaic image of a divinity with polos, scarf and necklace, who holds a bird in her right hand". Outstanding was the mass of small marble figurines which depict a female figure. The finds of the Hellenistic period, like the standing female figurines, were more numerous than those of the Archaic period (Fig. 90). Sherds of "Thracian" pottery, heads of female figurines of the Archaic period, bronze fibulae of the 7th century B.C., and one of the so-called "Phrygian" fibulae, a type popular in the islands toward the end of the 8th and beginning of the 7th century B.C., are reported from more recent surface collections. Trial excavation uncovered the ruins of a rectangular area of still uncertain date and of a small, single-aisled middle Byzantine chapel. To the east of the apse of the latter, the apse of a larger church, perhaps a small early Christian basilica, has been located. At the western part of the site, the area with the greatest concentration of surface finds, the deposits were disturbed and contained rich but detached material which dates from the 6th century B.C. to the 2nd century A.D. There is a striking number of fragments of Attic vases of the 5th and 4th centuries B.C. as well as examples of Corinthian pottery and that from eastern workshops (e.g. Middle Corinthian aryballoi, "Ionian" kylikes, etc.). There is

Photo Ch. Karadima

Fig. 90. Mandal' Panagia: Head of a terracotta Statuette.
Second Half of the 6th Century B.C.

also a notable amount of Hellenistic pottery. Among the other finds, of particular interest are inscribed sherds from dedicated kylikes of the 5th century B.C., a silver earring of the 4th century, an iron finger-ring, Hellenistic Samothracian coins, heads of Classical and Hellenistic female terracotta figurines, a drum (of Kybele?) from a terracotta figurine, etc. The investigation of the site is now at an early stage and the results which we now have at our disposal are limited, both for the Sanctuary itself and for its meaning in an area with such a strong religious life.

179

Selective Bibliography

The island of Samothrace:

I. Dragoumis, Σαμοθράκη, Athens, 1909 (German translation by R. Hampe, Potsdam, 1941).

S. N. Papageorgiou, Σαμοθράκη. Ιστορία του νησιού από τα πρώτα χριστιανικά χρόνια ως το 1914, Athens, 1982.

Important discussions of the Sanctuary:

Bouzek, J. and others, *Samothrace 1923, 1927, 1978. The Results of the Czechoslovak Excavations in 1927 conducted by A. Salač and J. Nepomucký and the Unpublished Results of the 1923 Franco-Czechoslovak Excavations conducted by A. Salač and F. Chapouthier*, Praha, 1985.

Deville, G. and Coquart, E., *Archives des missions scientifiques*, IV, 1867, pp. 253ff.

Conze, A. and others, *Archaeologische Untersuchungen auf Samothrake*, 2 vols., Vienna, 1875-1880.

Rubensohn, O., *Die Mysterienheiligtumer in Eleusis und Samothrake*, Berlin, 1892.

Fernand Chapouthier, Antoine Salač , Francois Salviat, "Le Theatre de Samothrace", *Bulletin de correspondence hellenique*, LXXX, 1956, pp. 118ff.

Lehmann, Phyllis Williams and Karl, *Samothracian Reflections, Aspects of the Revival of the Antique* (Bollingen Series XCII), Princeton, 1973, Chapters I, III.

The excavations of New York University:

Samothrace. Excavations Conducted by the Institute of Fine Arts, New York University. Karł Lehmann and Phyllis Williams Lehmann, Editors (Bollingen Series LX), in progress.

Vol. 1: *The Literary Sources.* Edited and Translated by Naphtali Lewis, New York, 1958.

Vol. 2, Part I: *The Inscriptions on Stone.* By P. M. Fraser,

New York, 1960.

Vol. 2, Part II: *The Inscriptions on Ceramics and Minor Objects.* By Karl Lehmann, New York, 1960.

Vol. 3: *The Hieron.* By Phyllis Williams Lehmann, Princeton, 1969.

Vol. 4, Part I: *The Hall of Votive Gifts.* By Karl Lehmann, New York, 1962.

Vol. 4, Part II: *The Altar Court.* By Karl Lehmann and Denys Spittle, New York, 1964.

Vol. 5: *The Temenos.* By Phyllis Williams Lehmann and Denys Spittle, Princeton, 1982.

Vol. 7: *The Rotunda of Arsinoe.* By James R. McCredie, Georges Roux, Stuart M. Shaw, and John Kurtich, Princeton, 1992.

Vol. 10: *The Propylon of Ptolemy II.* By Alfred K. Frazer, Princeton, 1990.

Vol. 11: *The Nekropoleis,* by Elsbeth B. Dusenbery, Princeton, 1998.

Preliminary reports and notices:

American Journal of Archaeology, XLIII, 1939, pp. 133ff; XLIV, 1940, pp. 485ff. *Hesperia,* XIX, 1950, p. 1ff; XX, 1951, pp. 1ff; XXI, 1952, pp. 19ff; XXII, 1953, pp. 1ff; XXIV, 1955, pp. 93ff. XXXIV, 1965, pp. 101ff; XXXVII, 1968, pp. 200ff; XLI, 1972, pp. 463ff; XLIII, 1974, pp. 454ff; XLIV, 1975, pp. 234ff; XLVII, 1978, pp. 211ff; XLVIII, 1979, pp. 1ff.; LXI, 1992, pp. 501 ff. *Archaeology,* I, 1948, pp. 44ff; VI, 1953, pp. 30ff; VII, 1954, pp. 91ff; XII, 1959, pp. 163ff; XVII, 1964, pp. 185ff; XX, 1967, pp. 116ff. *Bulletin de correspondance hellenique,* LXXXVI, 1962, pp. 268ff. *Journal of Glass Studies,* IX, 1967, pp. 34ff.

Lehmann, Phyllis Williams, *Skopas in Samothrace,* Smith College, Northampton, Massachusetts, 1973.

Inscriptions:
Corpus Inscriptionum Graecarum (Inscriptions Graecae), vol.
XII, part 8, Berlin, 1909, pp. 36ff.

The Samothracian cult:
Burkert, W., "Concordia discors: the literary and the archae-
ological evidence on the sanctuary of Samothrace", *Greek
Sanctuaries: New Approaches*, ed. N. Marinatos and R.
Hägg, London and New York, 1993, pp. 178 ff.
Cole, S., *Theoi Megaloi: The Cult of the Great Gods at Sa-
mothrace*, Leiden, 1984.
Hemberg, B., *Die Kabiren*, Uppsala, 1950, pp. 49ff.

The excavations outside the Sanctuary:
Preliminary reports:
The Archaeological Work in Macedonia and Thrace (AEMTH):
1, 1987 [1988], 499-502· 6, 1992 [1995], 677-84· 7, 1993 [1997],
647-55· 9, 1995 (in press).

Articles:
Chr. Karadima, «Βόρεια νεκρόπολη Σαμοθράκης. Η λίθινη
σαρκοφάγος 92.Τ9». *Ελληνιστική κεραμική από το Αιγαίο*.
Mytilini 1994, 196-205.
Chr. Karadima, «Εργαστήριο παραγωγής αμφορέων στη
Σαμοθράκη». *Γ´ Επιστημονική Συνάντηση για την Ελληνι-
στική Κεραμική. Χρονολογημένα Σύνολα-Εργαστήρια. 24-
27 September 1991 Thessaloniki*, Athens 1994, 355-62.
Chr. Karadima, «Ταφικά σύνολα ελληνιστικής κεραμικής
από τη Σαμοθράκη». *Δ´ Επιστημονική Συνάντηση για την
Ελληνιστική Κεραμική. Mytilini, March 1994*. Athens 1997,
381-4.
D. Matsas, «Μικρό Βουνί Σαμοθράκης: «Μια προϊστορική
κοινότητα σ' ένα νησιώτικο σύστημα του ΒΑ Αιγαίου», *Αν-
θρωπολογικά 6* (1984), 73-94.
D. Matsas, «Samothrace and the North-eastern Aegean: The
Minoan Connection», *Studia Troica 1* (1991), 159-79.

D. Matsas, «Minoan Long-Distance Trade: a View from the Northern Aegean», in Laffineur, R. and W.-D. Niemeier, (eds.), *Politeia. Society and State in the Aegean Bronze Age. Proceedings of the 5th International Aegean Conference, University of Heidelberg, Archäologisches Institut, 10-13 April 1994.* Liège 1995, 235-47.

Acknowledgements

Photographs:

Figs. 2, 3, 9, 11, 14, 15, 16, 17, 18, 19, 24, 25, 31, 33, 46, 55, 56, 59, 60, 66, 69, 70, 72, 76: Anna Wachsmann

Figs. 8, 10, 58, 73, 77, 78, 79: Alison Frantz

Figs. 39, 65, 67, 68, 75: Elsbeth B. Dusenbery

Figs. 12, 41, 42, 45, 47, 54, 57, 61, 62, 63, 64, 71, 74, 80: James R. McCredie

Frontispiece, Figs. 1, 4, 38: Nicholas D. Ohly

Fig. 22: E. and W. Myers

Figs. 6, 34: Phyllis W. Lehmann

Fig. 5: Giraudon

Fig. 7: Oxford, Bodleian Library

Fig. 81-85: D. Matsas

Fig. 87-90: Chr. Karadima

Drawings:

Fig. 20: Stuart M. Shaw

Fig. 37: S. D. T. Spittle

Fig. 35: Martin R. Jones

Fig. 36: Charles E. Brown

Fig. 40: Alfred K. Frazer

Fig. 53: Philip Oliver-Smith

Fig. 48: Nicholas D. Ohly

Figs. 23, 26, 27, 28, 29, 30, 32, 43, 44, 49, 50, 51, 52: John Kurtich

Fig. 86: D. Matsas

Plans I-IV: John Kurtich

Printed by Athanasios A. Altintzis
38, Ethnikis Aminis Str. • Gr-546 21 Thessaloniki
Tel. (031) 221.529, 222.965 • Fax (031) 242.440